THE WOODPECKER GOSPEL

BY
CARL O. COOPER

Introduction

This story would be classified by most readers as fiction. But these things, for the most part, really happened. The names have been changed, and the events and details have been rearranged and altered to a degree in order to make the people involved undetectable as much as is possible. There may be people who read this who are actually a part of this story themselves, but I think, in most cases, they cannot be absolutely sure. At least, that is my intent.

Carl O. Cooper

Contents ... Page 1

Contents ... Page 1

Philippians 2:12 (NKJV)
12 Therefore, my beloved, as you have always obeyed, not as in my presence only, but now much more in my absence, work out your own salvation with fear and trembling;

Chapter 1   The Beginning

I met Jay Thomas Finney when we attended the 6th grade together. We were a lot alike, actually, and we became close friends quickly. Jay Thomas had a mysterious way about him that quickly turned me into a willing companion. He could create wonderful mechanical designs on a piece of notebook paper that I feel sure would have no doubt turned the mechanical world upside down if any of them had ever been built. And he was a master at secret codes. We would spend hours creating secret codes and writing messages to each other and making each other solve the codes to understand the messages. What great adventures we shared. Jay Thomas could design animal traps and create the ideas and designs and I was his willing companion and laborer as we constructed his designs in the woods. We caught rabbits and squirrels and all kinds of small animals and varmints.

We were two of a kind, Jay Thomas and me. We were two backwoods Appalachian boys; ragged and poor but happy. The Coopers and the Finneys were part of an almost forgotten generation of people where time and progress moved slow.

The schoolhouse at Forest Hill Elementary school was set in the foothills of the Chilhowee Mountain in East Tennessee. We lived in the foothills. There was no flat level land anywhere close to where we lived and we owned no land. Those people who were fortunate enough to own land of their own were small farmers and usually raised just enough produce and fruit to make enough of a crop to get through the winter, and most had some type of supplemental income that helped their family to live. Some cut crossties and pulpwood and some worked as laborers for those who did.

But no one that I actually knew was so bad off that they were hungry and went without. We made it and our needs were simple. In fact, if you had asked Jay Thomas and me, we would have never believed that we were poor. In fact, it would have offended our parents if anyone had suggested that.

We owned no land and we farmed other people's land for shares, but we were happy.

Jay Thomas was worse off than I was in material things, since he lived with his mother and sister and his father had died some years before. We really never discussed things like that in the world we lived in. We spent every minute we had together in some great adventure and in exploring the creeks and rivers and mountains and woods around our houses in the foot hills of the Great Smokey Mountains.

My family owned no land and any land I walked on always belonged to someone else. We raised what food we needed and mama canned and dried all she could put up. My daddy worked for the Alcoa Aluminum Company and raised tobacco on shares for the man we rented our house from. Daddy was a farmer. He had no other real trade. Even for the Aluminum Company he worked on their farm. The Aluminum Company always had their own farm on the land the Company owned. I always suspected that they raised cattle not for profit but to show everyone that their plant did not harm the environment.

We had a mule and we used it to work our fields and garden and we had chickens and pigs. Somehow we always seemed to have one or two milk cows and other assorted animals which I always became attached to as pets even though daddy tried his best to make me treat them as farm animals.

Neither Jay Thomas nor I had very many restrictions on us as to how far we could go when we explored the mountains or what we were allowed to do. Our parents loved us just like all parents do, but it was a different time and kids had more freedom to come and go in those days and many of the chores and responsibilities we had carried an element of risk and danger to them as well. I was expected to keep the wood box filled for mama's cook stove and that meant using an ax to chop the wood. I had been splitting stove wood every day for the cook stove since I was in the first grade. I was expected to hook up the mules and plow just like my daddy and my older brother, Clifton. I fed and tended to the stock and the animals and basically I was expected to help with anything the adult men were expected to do. Not only did this give me extra skills to survive, it gave me confidence that I could. There were few things that I feared. We had superstitions and I feared those. And I had heard about the devil and hell, and I feared those. But by and large, Jay Thomas and I were free to come and go when and wherever we chose, providing our work at home was caught up and done.

In the spring of the 6th grade we found a wooden row boat half sunk in the edge of the Little Calf River. We figured the boat had floated off the mountain up near Cades Cove and finally hung up in the roots of the trees and sunk.

We wrestled and worked for 2 days to get this heavy, water logged boat out of the water and on to the bank in the dry. We worked every day after school. Luckily the boat had no holes in it and it dried out by its self after a couple of weeks in the dry. It was a great adventure to salvage this boat. We had great fun with the project but the boat itself was not that useful. It was so heavy and hard to manage on the river current that is was all two boys could do to keep it under control. We had to tie a rope on the bow and tie it to a log in the river to prevent it from floating on down the river with us in it. We could have managed it going down the river until it hit the Perry's Mill rapids and the dam but by then we would have had to abandon it to the currents and we would have lost our boat. I wasn't afraid of the river, we were always there, but I was not stupid either. However, things changed for the worse.

Jay Thomas' sister was 9 years old and J. Thomas had told her about the boat. Nothing would do her but to see it. Normally, Jay Thomas would never have taken his sister on an adventure to the river with him but this Saturday I had chores to do and we were setting out tobacco. I was expected to be a major part of this part of our tobacco crop and there was no way I would have even asked to skip work on a day like this. Many times Jay Thomas would help with this job but today, for whatever reason, Jay Thomas took his little sister to the river. I never saw her alive after this.

The river was up and the current was swift because of a rain in the cove and the high national park. This was nothing unusual. The high mountain rains were common in the spring and sometimes the river overflowed its banks. It really wasn't that bad today but the current was swift. Jay Thomas wrestled with the boat trying to pull it out of the water with the rope and it was hard to pull against the current but at last he pulled it up on the bank and when he sat down and looked around for his sister, Jen, she was not to be found.

The community was called out and we all looked and someone thought that she was taken by a tramp or wandered off into the woods and lost her way. But deep down, we all knew the river took her. People just mentioned these other things to give some glimmer of hope to the family that she might still be alive. Six days later her body was found hung up in the tree roots on the other side of Perry's Mill dam in the rapids. She was found by some kids walking on the river bank looking for a place to fish.

Things changed for Jay Thomas after that. We were still friends and companions but I saw a change in his behavior to a certain degree. At first it was sadness and grief but that begin to change. His mother was taking it hard and she was alone and she was trying to take care of herself and Jay Thomas, and no doubt it was hard. Neighbors could see the struggle and some wanted to help.

Mr. Waters lived about 4 miles down Ridge Road and he was what we would call a rich, successful neighbor. At least that's how I pictured him. He had one of these big fat type mail boxes and to me that was a sign of success. He had one of the few tractors from Montvale Springs to Maryville and his place always looked well tended. I liked him. He was always friendly to all of us kids. He offered to take me and Jay Thomas to church.

Now I had never been to church. I don't think Jay Thomas had ever been either. I had heard about the church of Christ and my grandpa was known for being a part of it, but my family had never attended any church. I had come close to going one time. I was in the edge of the cemetery of the Forest Hill Baptist church picking up black walnuts one fall day and I met the preacher's kid who was about my age. We hit it off pretty quick and he wanted me to come to church that Sunday with him. I thought I might just do that and so I ask daddy if I could go with that boy to church. Daddy was against it. He said since I had no church clothes to wear that I would look out of place if I showed up dressed like a farm boy with all these people with Sunday clothes on. His words convinced me and I figured he was right.

Well, Mr. Waters convinced us that our clothes would be Ok as long as they were clean and so we went.

Church was a mysterious place. I sensed that this must be a place where God would be. Everything was so royal and majestic and there was the strange organ music that played tunes that I couldn't even begin to describe and had never heard. Church scared me. I was awed and afraid of this palace of a place. I sat there and looked at the people dressed in their finest and the men had on neck ties and the women had on special Sunday hats and some of them had white gloves that covered their hands and extended up almost to their elbows. I sat quiet and still and I could see that Jay Thomas was acting just about like me. The preacher got up to talk and at first he used a normal voice but as he seemed to gain confidence his voice began to take on a strange loud excitement. The voice would alternate between soft and loud and he would take these loud breaths in between words. It seemed that he spoke so hard and loud that he was so out of breath it was all he could do to preach. I was awed and amazed at all the things that I saw for the first time that day. Not many things would have scared me, but this did. Surely God was in this place right here.

We left church and Mr. Waters took us to our houses in his car. This was Sunday and Jay Thomas was not at school the next day. After school daddy had left word for me to split up a huge pile of wood he had sawed into short logs while I was at school. Daddy was working the second shift at the plant and he worked around the house during most of the day and at the plant's farm until 10:00 at night. We never owned a car and so he caught the work bus to work about 2 and worked until he could ride it home at night.

It took me all of Monday afternoon until dark to split that pile of wood and I never had time to go check on Jay Thomas that day. Jay Thomas was not at school on Tuesday either. By now I knew something was wrong.

After school I walked the 2 miles to Jay Thomas' house. There were few telephones in those days and none of the people I knew even had one.

By the time I was close enough to Jay Thomas' house to see it; I could see a car in the yard in front of the house. This was most unusual because like the Coopers, the Finneys did not own a car either. As I walked up on to the front porch I was greeted by a woman in a white starched dress with a strange white cap of sorts on her head. I had seen pictures of nurses and I knew she was a nurse but why was she here in Jay Thomas' house.

I was told to stay away from the house because it was under quarantine. There was a yellow sign tacked up on the front door and it said, "Quarantine". I had never heard the word "Polio" before but I could tell it was serious. My friend Jay Thomas had polio.

Chapter 2   My Life Changed

Jay Thomas did not make it back to school at Forest Hill Elementary. It was several years before I saw him again. I watched him and his mother move out of their little house on Ridge Road. I knew they couldn't afford to live there anymore. There was nothing I could do. What could a kid my age do, except watch it happen and hurt. I spent many days sitting behind our smokehouse by myself and crying for Jay Thomas and for the loneliness I felt in my life.

Jay Thomas was brought out and placed into the back of a black "hearse like" ambulance by two men who were wearing suits and ties. He was strapped in a contraption made out of iron and it almost looked like a coffin with the part around the head missing. They called it an iron lung. I never actually knew how it worked but I knew it was keeping Jay Thomas alive.

I watched the ambulance drive out of the yard and head down the gravel road toward town. I watched the dust boil up behind it and block the vision of the vehicle and I could not move or take my eyes off the cloud. The dust slowly settled on the ragweed and goldenrod along the side of the road and the ambulance was out of sight. Jay Thomas was gone and he was no longer a part of my life. I ran all the way home and I hid for the rest of the day behind the smokehouse alone.

There was sadness in my life without Jay Thomas. It must have been noticed by the people around me because the school teacher, Mrs. Huskey, asked me to stay after school one afternoon and wanted to know if everything was alright with my family at home. It was years later when I remembered this and I finally understood why she did it.

Mr. Waters stopped by our house one Saturday and he talked with my daddy about coming to church. Daddy was never persuaded to go to church as long as he lived, but he seemed to know that I needed something and so he mentioned it to me and I agreed to go.

Church was a turning point in my life without Jay Thomas. I knew many of the kids who were there and they greeted me as though I was part of their group. I quickly felt at ease, almost as though I belonged. From that point on, I felt comfortable at this church. I blended in with the other young people and I fit in.

Church services, on the other hand, were always fearful to me. Something always seemed strange and mysterious about this place. God must be here somewhere. The preacher said we needed God in our lives and yet, somehow, I just could not feel the presence of God in me. What was wrong with me?

Sometimes while the preacher, Reverend Milsaps, was speaking, members of the congregation would be overcome with the "Holy Spirit" and stand up and give testimony about their own lives. Others were quick to shout out "amen" and "hallelujah" and some would even cry. I wanted to feel the presence of God in me, but something was wrong. Why was I so different? Was I so bad that God had no interest in me? I feared hell and somehow I felt I was destined to everlasting fire.

Even with these feelings I found a place in that Baptist church. I could not find a comfortable place in the religious part of the church but the association with the youth group gave me a sense of belonging.

By the time I entered the 7th grade I had acclimated to the Victory Baptist Church. Jay had been gone about a year and I needed these other kids in my life. The church sent us on trips together in the church bus and I had great times on these outings.

Anita was a friendly young girl about my age and she was almost always on these church outings with her brother Tim. Try as best I could, I could never bring myself to be comfortable around her because she was a girl. I was not comfortable around girls my own age. She took an interest in me and seemed to seek me out every chance she got. One outing for the youth group involved sitting around a bonfire at night and sure enough, Anita sat down right beside me. Now I can't say that I didn't want her to sit there, because I really did. But I was uncomfortable and it was hard for me to talk to girls. And this time Anita said something to me that changed the way I looked at religion for all time. "Have you been baptized?" she asked.

"Baptized?" I said. "Well, no. Have you?"

"Sure, almost everyone in the group our age has been baptized."

"Why?" I asked. "Why are people baptized?"

"It shows people that you are a Christian and that you have accepted Christ."

"I thought I was a Christian," I said. "What do you mean when you say you have accepted Christ?"

Anita thought for a minute and said this, "Well, you really ought to talk to Reverend Milsaps about that but it really just means that you have accepted Jesus as your personal Savior and you have let Him come into your heart and save you."

"Did Jesus come into your heart?" I asked.

"Sure He did," she said.

"How did you know when He came in?" I asked.

"Well, I just felt His presence," she said "and when I felt the presence of the Holy Spirit, I prayed that Jesus would come into my heart and forgive me of my sins, and He did."

"You felt the presence of the Holy Spirit?" I said. "How did you know it was the Holy Spirit?"

"I just knew. You can tell."

"I haven't felt that," I said. "Or if I did I couldn't tell."

"Don't you want to be saved?" she said.

"Yes I do," I said. "I want to be saved."

"Then pray for Jesus to come into your heart, and He will."

"I'll pray harder," I said. "But I don't seem to feel the Holy Spirit like other people in the church do."

"You ought to talk to Reverend Milsaps." she said. "He can help you with all of this."

Anita's words went through my head for days after that and it caused a great fear to overcome me about the condition of my soul. If what she says is right and I am the only kid my age that has not been saved and baptized, then something must be wrong with me. Why has the Holy Spirit not contacted me like it did them?

For the next 2 weeks my whole family was in the field cutting our tobacco crop. We raised Kentucky Burley tobacco and unlike the short stalk tobacco grown in the east, Kentucky Burley is tall. Some of the tobacco plants we raised were taller than a man could reach to touch the top of the plant. We didn't prime off the leaves and put the "hands of tobacco" in flue cure barns to dry. Instead, we cut down the entire stalk and speared it on a tobacco stick along with about 5 or 6 other stalks and the entire stick was hung on tiers of racks constructed in our barns to air cure for market. By November these tobacco stalks were dried out and the leaves were a golden brown. On a dry day with low humidity the tobacco leaves would be brittle and the slightest touch would shred a leaf to dusty powder. But on a damp humid day, especially if it was drizzling rain, you could handle the leaves and they were as limber as dishrags in your hand. On a day like this we referred to the tobacco as being "in case". And on these types of days we stripped the leaves off the stalks and graded the tobacco into piles of the same color. These leaves were tied up into "hands" and placed on a flat, lattice type of a carrier to take to market. We depended on the money we got for this tobacco to get us through the winter. It was always a rush to try to sell the tobacco before Christmas. I guess what little we could afford for Christmas came from the money we got for the sale of the tobacco.

Raising tobacco is frowned on today; especially by Christian people. Today we know the health hazards that come from smoking tobacco but this was unknown in those days and raising tobacco in East Tennessee and even smoking was so common that it was done by almost everyone I knew.

Mr. Waters had stopped picking me up for church after I started the 7th grade. The church used a church bus to pick up people in the area now and I could ride the bus. Once in a while my mama would ride the bus with me and we would both go. But this was rare and she usually stayed home with daddy.

Anita was always there and each time I saw her I seemed to become just a little more at ease in her presence. She was pretty and flirty and she was at ease around every boy at church but she seemed to seek me out. Nothing else was mentioned about me being baptized or about me being saved. I think Anita must have mentioned it to someone though, because not many Sundays after our talk, Mr. Waters asked me if I would ride home with him from church. Naturally I agreed. I had no idea that he wanted to talk to me about my salvation.

On the way home in the car Mr. Waters brought up the subject of the church. "Carl, there's something I've been wanting to ask you."

"What's that?" I said.

"Do you feel like you're saved." he said.

"To tell you the truth, it's been bothering me some. I've talked to some of the other kids in the youth group and they tell me that I need to take Jesus into my heart and I'll be saved. Anita told me that I would feel it happen and I would know when Jesus came into my heart. But I really haven't felt that way, as far as I can tell."

"Have you ever felt like the Holy Spirit was working inside you, Carl?"

"I don't know. Is that when Jesus comes into your heart?"

"Well, the Holy Spirit comes into your heart first and He convinces you that you are lost and that you need salvation. Men won't seek salvation until the Holy Spirit comes into their heart and enlightens their understanding of Spiritual things."

"Well, I have been thinking that I was lost and need salvation," I said.

"Then the Holy Spirit must be working inside you right now," Mr. Waters replied. "Have you prayed the sinner's prayer?"

"No, I don't think I have. Is that what I need to do to be saved?"

"Carl, once the Holy Spirit has convinced you that you are lost, He allows you to have faith enough in Jesus to be saved. If you have faith in Jesus you can pray the sinner's prayer."

"How do you pray the sinner's prayer?" I asked.

"Simple, all you have to do is to ask Jesus to come into your life and forgive you of your sins and you'll be saved."

"You mean if I pray that prayer I'll be saved? Is that all anyone has to do?"

"That's all there is to it," he said. "If the Holy Spirit is working inside you and telling you that you need to be saved, then you are one of the ones God has chosen for salvation since long before you were born and you couldn't be lost even if you wanted to. God is telling you what you need to do."

"Could I do that any time?" I asked.

"Why don't you do it now," he said. "You can say these words; *Lord Jesus, come into my heart and save me, I pray.*"

"OK, I will," I said. "Lord Jesus, come into my heart and save me, I pray."

"Young man, you made a great choice today. You've become a Christian and you're saved. This is a moment you'll never forget as long as you live. Next Sunday I'll talk to Reverend Milsaps about this and we will see about getting you baptized."

"Mr. Waters, what am I supposed to feel now that I am a Christian?" Anita said I would feel the Holy Spirit inside me. How will I know when that happens?"

"Don't worry son, the Holy Spirit is in you working right now. You'll feel Him."

By this time we were at my house and Mr. Waters pulled into the yard and we said our goodbyes. I watched the car lumber down the gravel road that ran in front of our house and the image faded into the dust that boiled up behind the car until it was lost from view. What had just happened to me, I thought? Mr. Waters said I was saved. He seems to be a man who knows about God. I must be.

Chapter 3   Old Bad Eye

Our house was a simple plain structure of unpainted wood. It wasn't much but it was all I had ever known. We were about 4 miles up a rural gravel road called Pea Ridge Road. I never knew why this road had this name. We grew a few peas in our garden but nobody grew enough to name a road. Pea Ridge started at the Montvale Road and ran 4 miles to our house and about 3 more miles to Frank Hall's country store. Frank Hall would buy eggs from me when I could find any and he would pay about 35 cents for a dozen. A soft drink or a candy bar would cost a nickel each and 35 cents would buy a drink and a candy bar, 25 long rifle 22 shells, and a Superman or a Tarzan of the Apes comic book.

Our house had 4 rooms and a "lean to" room built on the back that we called a junk room and we had a front and a back porch. There were no closets and each room had a light bulb that dangled from a cord attached to the ceiling of each room. There were no bathrooms or running water in the house and our water came from a well between the house and the barn. Our heat was simple enough. We had a coal circulator in the living room and mama cooked our food on a wood cook stove. One of my jobs was to keep wood and coal in the boxes beside the stoves. I always had what mama called my "night work." Every day before dark I had to carry in 2 buckets of fresh water from the well and cut kindling for tomorrow's fires and make sure that the boxes were filled with stove wood and coal.

There were no foundation walls for the house to sit on and it sat on rock pillars that held it about 2 to 3 feet off the ground. You could get on your knees and see all the way from one side to the other under the house.

The chickens and the cat always loved this spot where it was cool and dry and dusty. The floors of the house were made out of rough planks that were somewhat close together but in many places I could lay down on my stomach on the floor and I could look down between the cracks in the floor and see the chickens walking around under the house and I could listen to the contented ones "sing". A chicken will sometimes make a noise that sounds like they are "singing" when they are not alarmed and are sitting in the shade.

The room we called a junk room was really just a room that had been added on for a place to store our chicken feed and corn meal in the dry. The room always had a smell of corn and grain and I can still sometimes smell that aroma in places and it brings pleasant memories to flood the senses of my mind.

There was an outdoor toilet about 50 yards from the back of the house in the edge of the woods. This walk was a spooky and fearful walk at night. There were tales of things that lived in the woods and there were bears and wildcats that were real. But mostly, there were the radio dramas in the night. "Suspense" and "The screeching Door" brought fear to everyone's life at night. And if scary radio programs were not enough, there was a genuine fear of superstitious things and tales told by those adults in our lives who really believed what they feared.

But I have wonderful memories of these days in this old house on Pea Ridge Road. It wasn't much of a house as I look back on it but I really didn't think about that at the time. I remember the grapes that always grew on the sagging wire fence that bordered the back of our yard. I remember the apple trees that grew in the little orchard across the gravel road where mama's vegetable garden was always planted. I remember the trails I cut through the woods up and down the hills for my homemade coaster wagons. I remember the creek and the dammed up swimming hole. I remember the big maple trees that grew on the edge of the bank that bordered the gravel road. I would climb these trees in the summer and hang out over the road and watch the cars go down the gravel road right under me and not even know I was there. I would pretend to be a big leopard or a great ape just ready to pounce on them before they knew I was there. I loved this old house and I have wonderful memories of the life I lived as a boy.

I had a dog. I don't really know what kind of a dog he was and I can't even say where he came from. I got up one morning and went out on the back porch, and he was there. He was hungry and friendly and he was eat up with the mange. I didn't know what caused the mange but I knew it when I saw it and I knew how to cure it. I fed him for a few days and when it looked like he was bound to stay with me, I soaked him in motor oil from a can we kept out in the barn. This was our common cure for skin infections of our animals. Motor oil and kerosene were common medicines in those days along with turpentine and salt.

He was a small white dog with some black spots and patches around his ears and one eye. He had one eye with a large black spot around it and the other one was white. Daddy called him a "feist". I tried to think of a name for him for a while and considered several, but then someone looked at the one black eye and the name "Bad Eye" seemed to somehow "just fit."

So the name stuck. From then on, he was "Bad Eye" to all of us.

He was a good squirrel dog and he seemed to come to us with the ability to tree squirrels even with no training from me. Maybe somebody else trained him but he already could do it when he came to live with me.

I loved the dog and it was obvious that he loved me. We were constant companions. Bad Eye was always there when I left for school and he was always there when I got home. He greeted me with enthusiasm and excitement and pure love for me as his friend. And I loved him the same way.

Edgar Watkins was a young boy about my same age. He was in my grade at school and we saw each other every day at school. He lived about 3 miles on down Pea Ridge Road just a few hundred yards past Frank Hall's Grocery Store. I really had not had too much contact with Edgar until I met him as part of the youth group at Victory Baptist church. Since that time we had been good friends and spent many hours together finding adventures in the fields and woods around our houses. Edgar wanted to go to the river and he wanted me to go with him.

We planned to spend Saturday fishing the Little Calf River. During the week we dug red worms for our bait and got our fishing gear ready. Our "fishing gear" consisted of a small metal Prince Albert tobacco can with some assorted fishhooks, sinkers and line. And I had a worn out leather creel that been around our house as long as I could remember and I had about 6 assorted floats in it along with the Prince Albert can and line. There was no reason to have a fishing pole because we always cut new poles from the tall river cane that grew plentiful all along the banks of the river. We each had chores to do on Saturday but the plan was to meet about noon at Roger Blair's pasture gate and walk the trail to the river.

Saturday morning seemed normal enough at first. But by the time I had fed the animals and carried two wash tubs full of water from the well for mama to wash clothes I began to notice something that was not quite right. Bad Eye was not following at my side as he usually did. I called his name and I whistled for him but he still did not come. I finished my work and got my fishing gear ready to leave and I looked under the house. Sure enough, Bad Eye was lying in the dust. When I spoke to him and called his name he wagged his tail and he got up and came out from under the house. He seemed happy enough and he followed me as I took off across the road.

I met Edgar at the pasture gate and we walked the 2 miles to the river and we each made a careful selection of the poles we would choose for our personal fishing pole. Choosing the right pole was important and was not something to be hasty about. The right pole had to be long and light but it also had to be limber and strong. The pole had to give with the tug and weight of a fish but it must not break or all would be lost. The fish would be gone but worse than that, the sinker and the hook would be gone as well. We didn't have many hooks and we sure didn't want to lose one.

We caught several fish. They were Catfish and Brim. We never caught Trout or Bass. Sometimes we might catch a Crappie or a Sucker but we considered the sucker just a trash fish and not worth the trouble to take it home. Most of the Brim were too small to eat and so we turned them loose but we had about 6 pretty good size Catfish that would be about a mess for one table. I told Edgar he could have the fish and so we made ready to go home about 4 or 5 in the afternoon. We retrieved our fishing gear and stashed our poles in the cane thicket and made ready to leave.

"Where is Bad Eye?" I said.

"You know, I haven't seen him in a pretty good while." Edgar replied. "I thought I saw him trying to get a drink out of the river some time ago. Hold on, I'll walk down to that rock where he was at."

"Carl, come down here!" he exclaimed. "Bad Eye's under this ledge and he looks like he's sick or something."

"Look at his mouth. He looks like he must have got hold of a toad frog. His mouth is foaming like he tried to eat a frog."

Edgar walked closer to Bad Eye to get a closer look and suddenly the dog snarled and growled and the hair on the back of his neck stood straight up and Edgar stopped in his tracks.

"Something is wrong with this dog, Carl. He acts like he would bite me."

"Bad Eye won't bite anybody," I said. "Get back and let me see what's wrong."

I stepped closer to Bad Eye to get a better look and suddenly he leaped up on his feet and tried to lunge at me with the same fierce actions he had with Edgar. The only thing that kept him from biting me was that he was so unsteady on his feet that he fell side to side and it looked like he could not move his back legs. There was a foaming froth coming from his mouth and it was plain to see that Bad Eye was sick.

"Edgar, Bad Eye is sick," I said. "We've got to help him somehow. We've got to do something."

"Get away from him, Carl. Bad Eye's not just sick. Bad Eye's gone mad. He's got rabies. Let's get out of here before he bites one of us. We've got to go tell somebody about this."

We ran from the river. I was so afraid of the stories I had heard about mad dogs and rabies that I didn't have time to think about what was happening to Bad Eye, my friend.

We must have run all the way to my house and we found daddy at the woodpile smoking his pipe and sitting on the chop block resting. Daddy's eyes lit up when we told him what we had just seen. We waited while he loaded the 22 rifle and came back out of the house.

"You boys show me where he's at," he said.

We made our way back to the river and it was just before sundown when we made it to the spot where Bad Eye was last seen. He was still there.

"I see him," daddy said. "He's not moving. I think he's dead. You boys stay up here and I'm going closer to get a better look. No matter what happens, don't let any part of that dog touch you in any way. Rabies will kill you and there's not any cure for it as far as I know."

As daddy stepped down the bank into the gravels of the river, Bad Eye raised his head. He was weak and his mouth still had the foaming froth slobber all over his face, but when he saw us this time his tail wagged in a friendly way. Suddenly my heart was broken for my friend. Daddy raised the gun to his shoulder and I saw the flash as the bullet left the barrel of the gun. There were two more shots and Bad Eye jerked when the first 2 struck his head but the third shot fell on a lifeless body and Bad Eye was dead.

There was little said on the walk home. There was nothing to say. Daddy did what had to be done. But it hurt.

I didn't even try to go to church the next day. Nothing was mentioned about the dog and everybody just pitched in and did my chores for me without saying anything. I remember sitting behind the smokehouse for a long time by myself. I loved that dog and I know he loved me. I'll never forget him as long as I live.

Chapter 4 The Baptism

It was two more weeks before I went back to Victory Baptist church. Anita and Edgar and the whole youth group seemed to welcome me back and made me feel like I was a part of their group. Anita and Edgar sat down beside me before class started and Anita said, "I heard you were born again. Reverend Milsaps came into our class last Sunday looking for you."

"What did he want?" I asked.

"He told us you were saved and he wanted to talk to you about being baptized."

"Well, Mr. Waters took me home from church a few weeks ago and he told me that I needed to say a prayer and I would be saved. He told me what to say."

"Did you say the sinner's prayer?"

"Yes, he told me it was the sinner's prayer and he told me that Jesus would come into my heart."

"Well, that makes you a born again Christian."

"What do you mean born again?" I asked. Anita was answering all the questions but I could see that Edgar was just as interested in the answers as I was. He seemed to be just as confused about this as I was even though he had been baptized at the same time she was, along with several others from the group.

"Born again means that you have a new life, it means that when you're saved the Holy Spirit works inside you to make you a new person. Look at how many questions you've asked me, Carl. The old person you were before you were saved had a sinful nature and you couldn't understand the Bible and things like that. But now that you've been saved you'll begin to understand all these things. The Holy Spirit will work inside you to make you understand. So that means you're born again."

Edgar spoke up, "What about me? Does that mean I'm born again, too?"

"Sure it does. You've been saved and you were baptized, too."

"I don't feel like I understand so much," Edgar said.

"That's sort of how I feel, too," I said; speaking more to Edgar than Anita. "I sort of thought I would be able to feel different when the Holy Spirit came in to me. It's not exactly how I thought it would be."

"Maybe you boys need to talk to Reverend Milsaps," Anita said.

Before we could answer, the bell began to ring to start the class.

The teacher for the Sunday School class for our age group was Bill Robinson. He was a good man and I liked him. He went with us on most of the outings and trips the youth group took and his wife, Judy, was well liked by Anita and the other girls in the class. They were in their mid thirties and they had no children as of yet. In truth, they had just as much fun on the trips as the rest of us did. They loved the outdoors and the games and they fit right in with the group.

Today the question was already on my mind as it must have been on Edgar's as well, and Edgar said, "Mr. Robinson, can you tell us what it means to be born again?"

"Well Edgar, let's see. That's not in our quarterly today, is it?"

"No, I don't think so. But we were just talking about it just now. Carl was saved and Anita said he was born again. We were just wondering about that."

"Well I know what it means but I can't remember where in the Bible you find the story about it."

"Does anyone have a Bible with a concordance in it?"

"My Bible has one," one of the boys said. "What do you want me to look up?"

"Well, let's start by looking up born again," Mr. Robinson said. "Try that."

"It shows one place in John 3:3," the boy named Jerry said.

"I believe that's it. Read a few verses and let me see if that's what I'm thinking about."

Jerry read:

John 3:1-7 (NKJV)

1 *There was a man of the Pharisees named Nicodemus, a ruler of the Jews.*

2 *This man came to Jesus by night and said to Him, "Rabbi, we know that You are a teacher come from God; for no one can do these signs that You do unless God is with him."*

3 *Jesus answered and said to him, "Most assuredly, I say to you, unless one is born again, he cannot see the kingdom of God."*

4 *Nicodemus said to Him, "How can a man be born when he is old? Can he enter a second time into his mother's womb and be born?"*

5 *Jesus answered, "Most assuredly, I say to you, unless one is born of water and the Spirit, he cannot enter the kingdom of God.*

6 *That which is born of the flesh is flesh, and that which is born of the Spirit is spirit.*

7 *Do not marvel that I said to you, 'You must be born again.'*

"That's the one," Mr. Robinson said. "This will answer all your questions about being born again. Let's look at it."

"First off," Mr. Robinson said, "In the first verse you will see that Jesus is talking with Nicodemus. Nicodemus was one of the rulers of the Jews and he was a believer in Jesus. Verse 2 tells us that he must have been afraid of being a follower of Christ because he came to see Jesus at night. No doubt Jesus could see the fear in Nicodemus and he told him straight up that unless he was born again he couldn't go to heaven. Look at verse three. The Kingdom of God is the same as saying heaven."

"That makes sense," I thought to myself without speaking up.

Mr. Robinson went on to explain, "Verse 4 shows us that Nicodemus did not understand what Jesus meant when He said a man must be born again. He thought Jesus was talking about a physical birth like a baby being born. A lot of people today still don't understand this, but Jesus explains it in the next 2 verses. It's really simple but people today are just like Nicodemus and they twist it all up and try to put baptism in here and everything else. But look what Jesus says in verse 5. Unless one is born of the water and the spirit he cannot go to heaven."

"Mr. Robinson, why does it say you have to be baptized to enter the kingdom of God?" I said.

"Where do you see that, Carl?" he said.

"Well, it says it there in verse 5," I said. "It says unless you are born of the water and the Spirit you cannot enter the kingdom of God. That sounds like it's talking about baptism."

"Oh no, goodness no; that would make baptism required for salvation. You know that that's not right, don't you?"

"Well, I'm not sure. It seems to read like baptism is required if you want to go to heaven."

Edgar spoke up, "You know, it does seem to read like that here in verse 5. It looks like the water here is baptism."

"No it's not baptism. It can't be baptism because we know for sure that baptism does not save anyone."

"Look at a few verses down at what it says in John 3:16. You all know this verse."

John 3:16 (NKJV)

¹⁶ For God so loved the world that He gave His only begotten Son, that whoever believes in Him should not perish but have everlasting life.

"This verse is all we need to see in the Bible to tell us what we need to do in order to be saved. If this was all of the Bible we had it would be enough to tell us what is required to be saved."

"Yeah, I see what that verse says, but why does John 3:5 say we have to be born of water? That seems so obviously to be referring to baptism."

"Well we've already seen that it can't be baptism. Most people explain it like this; there are 2 types of births being described here. There is the physical birth which is described as occurring with water, which is how babies are born, and there is the Spiritual birth which is by the Spirit. Notice what it says in verse 6."

John 3:6 (NKJV)

6 That which is born of the flesh is flesh, and that which is born of the Spirit is spirit.

"See, this verse proves that there are 2 births referred to here. The fleshly birth and the Spiritual birth."

"Well, I see what it says here, but Nicodemus asked Jesus what it means to be born again and Jesus said that we have to be born of the water and the Spirit. It seems like Jesus meant that there were 2 steps in being born again, water and Spirit."

"Well, Carl, it sounds like you need to talk to reverend Milsaps on that one. But we need to get on with our lesson in this week's quarterly or we won't finish it."

After class was over, several of the kids, including Anita and Edgar surrounded me and asked me if I understood the passage we talked about in class. All of them except Edgar told me that the water in these verses was definitely not baptism. But Edgar asked me questions about it that seemed to indicate to me that he was just as confused about it as I was and neither one of us was fully convinced.

The main worship service of the church was just as majestic and royal and fearful this day as all other Sunday services were. I feared God in this place and as I sat there I felt guilty that I had had doubts about His word in class. What is wrong with me, I thought. God could strike me dead or let all types of evil things happen to me for the way I was acting about being saved. Somehow I must be preventing the Holy Spirit from coming into my life and helping me to understand what I need to know. I prayed silently and fearfully that God would help me to understand what I was doing wrong.

My thoughts drifted to Edgar and I wondered what was going through his mind. Could he be as afraid as I was? Something about his face seemed to say he was.

After church was over and the people were making their way out the door, Reverend Milsaps tried his best to greet them all and give a friendly shake to every person's hand he could reach. My turn came to greet the preacher and Reverend Milsaps grabbed my hand and enthusiastically said, "Carl, my boy, it's good to see you again today. I've been wanting to see you. I hear you need to be baptized."

"Well, I wanted to see you about that," I said.

If Reverend Milsaps had mentioned this about baptism on any other day than this day, right after the confusion about baptism in the Sunday school class, I would have known what he meant. But suddenly, I wasn't sure what he was referring to any more.

"Why don't you wait around a few minutes," he said. "After people leave I want to talk to you about being baptized."

"I can't wait too long," I said. "I have to ride the church bus home."

"Don't worry, I won't let him leave you. He'll wait."

While I was waiting Edgar said, "Are you going to get baptized?"

"I think so," I said. "How did you get baptized? How did they do it?"

"Well there's nothing to it, really. They took a bunch of us over to the college to the indoor swimming pool and they baptized us all at the same time."

"Were you afraid?"

"Some, but it really wasn't near as bad as I thought it would be. We all went into the shallow end of the pool and we waded out until we were about waist deep and one by one Reverend Milsaps dunked us all the way under the water and we came up and everybody clapped and said we could join the church if we wanted to. That's really all there was to it."

I heard Reverend Milsaps call my name from down the hall near his office and we went in and he sat behind his desk and motioned for me to sit in the chair.

"Well, Carl, are you ready to be baptized?"

"Well, I wanted to ask you about that. I just want to be sure I understand it. Maybe you can tell me about being saved. Do I need to be baptized in order to be saved?"

"My goodness no, baptism is not required to be saved. The Bible tells us that we are saved by faith alone. If you believe that Jesus is God's son and you take Him into your heart as your personal Savior, He will give you the free gift of Salvation."

"You mean all that's required is faith in Jesus, and nothing else?"

"That's all you need. If you were to try and add anything to that you would be adding something more than the Bible tells us we need. Faith alone is what the Bible tells us we need."

"Well I've had faith in Jesus ever since I was small. I've always believed in Jesus. But Mr. Waters told me I also needed to pray the sinner's prayer."

"Well, sure, you need to pray the sinner's prayer and ask Jesus to come into your heart. I understand you did that."

"Yes I did. Mr. Waters told me what to say. But he also said I needed the Holy Spirit to enter me and enlighten me so I could understand what to do in order to ask Jesus to come into my heart."

"Well that's pretty complicated for a young boy to understand, Carl. But don't worry about that. The Holy Spirit is working on you right now. You'll understand all of this in time. But right now we need to get you baptized."

Now there are 6 people waiting on baptism and I've been wanting to add your name to that list as soon as we can schedule a date at the college to reserve the pool. Do you want me to add you to that list or do you want to wait on the next group?"

"What do you think I should do? I just want to do what you think God would want me to do."

"I think you should go on and be baptized. Why wait? You can be baptized with this group in 2 weeks and it might be 2 months before another group is baptized."

"OK," I said. "I'll go with the group."

Two weeks were gone before I hardly knew it.

I had told daddy about what I was going to do and he had no advice as to what he thought I should do about being baptized. His only words about it were "Do whatever you think you want to do."

The day came and the baptism went off as scheduled. The actual baptism itself was pretty quick but the sermon and speeches leading up to it seemed to take forever. After the baptism was over we were all taken back to the church building in the church bus for dinner at the building. All in all it was a grand parade and celebration for the church. The pomp and celebration made the entire process seem so official and Godly in my sight that I was finally convinced that God was surely involved in this process and what I was doing was surely the way God wanted it to be.

As the summer went on I attended Victory Baptist Church on a regular basis. I had learned my lesson about speaking up in class. The longer I sat in church and listened, the more I just adapted to the teaching and environment where I was. I was acclimating to my surroundings and becoming comfortable with what I heard.

Chapter 5   **The Haircut**

Most of the time daddy cut my hair. He had a pair of hand held clippers that had been around the house ever since I had been alive. I dreaded haircuts. Daddy had a rhythm to his cutting strokes as he cut. He would snip, snip, snip and then flip the clippers and the loose hair and then snip, snip, snip again. Over and over he would use this rhythm. But it never failed, every 10 or 12 times his rhythm would get off and he would flip before the snip was finished and my hair would be yanked and that hurt. I dreaded that and I was quick to flinch even when it didn't happen.

I like to go to the barber shop and get my hair cut. And by the time I finished the 7th grade I would save my money so I could get my own hair cut. A haircut only cost 25 cents and I would pay that gladly.

The barber's name was Cordell. He was a relative of mine to some degree. He was my uncle Birch's brother. Cordell knew my daddy real well but I seldom ever saw him except when I decided to pay for a haircut. A Saturday came and I decided to have Cordell cut my hair.

There were several people in the barber shop when I arrived and one in the chair. This was no problem for me. I had plenty of time and I liked to sit around and listen to the conversations of the men waiting to get their hair cut. Most of the time, Cordell talked about religion. My daddy's family members were known to be members of the Church of Christ and all I had ever heard about that group was not good. They were known to be fanatics of some kind and they seemed to like to argue about the Bible. I was told at church that we should never argue about the Bible.

My time finally came to get in the chair and Cordell asked me how I wanted my hair cut, and I told him that I had been thinking about getting one of those flat tops that some of the boys had.

Cordell laughed, " Boy, your daddy would have my hide if I cut your hair like that. If you want a haircut like that you will have to have your daddy tell me it's OK."

"I don't see why I need his OK, it's my hair. Everybody at school is getting their hair cut like that."

"Not by me they're not. Not without their daddy's OK."

"What do you think about sideburns?" I said.

"Well, I'll tell you what, if you won't tell your daddy about it, I'll leave the sideburns this time. If he doesn't get on to me about it, we'll see about a little longer next time."

"OK, let's do it that way," I said.

As Cordell was putting the barber cape around my neck, he said, "Say Carl, I heard you were baptized."

"Yeah, I was. How did you hear about that?"

"Well, your buddy, Mr. Waters comes in here and get's his haircut and he told me about it. Why were you baptized?"

"What do you mean, why?"

"Well, were you baptized for the forgiveness of your sins?"

"Well, I'm not sure about that. I was told that I needed to be baptized because I was saved."

"You mean someone told you that you were saved before you were baptized? If that's the case, how did they tell you that you were saved?"

"Reverend Milsaps says that we are saved by faith alone and that's all the Bible tells us we need."

"Boy, I hate to tell you this, but if that's what you did, you're not saved at all. You still haven't done what the Bible tells you to do in order to be saved."

"Are you saying I'm not saved? I did what the preacher said I needed to do."

"Your preacher just doesn't know what he's talking about. Unless you are baptized for the right reason you're not saved."

"Cordell, I don't see how you can be right about that. Reverend Milsaps told me specifically that baptism was not required in order to be saved. He told me that the Bible tells us that we're saved by faith alone."

"Carl, you need to read your Bible. This stuff they're telling you at the Baptist church is all false doctrine."

"Well, I don't believe in arguing over the Bible. You have your church's teachings and other people have their church's teaching but what difference does it make anyway, since we are all going to the same place?" Those were not really my words, but I repeated what I had heard said by some of the men at church.

"Carl, do you have a Bible?"

"Mama has one at home. It's a great big one."

"Look here, I'm going to give you a Bible. This is a good one and it has maps and a concordance and references and everything. But I want you to promise me something."

"What do you mean? I don't know if daddy will allow me to take a Bible free."

"Well, this is different. I'll talk to him about that. But I have 2 verses of Scripture I want you to look up and tell me what you think when you come in the next time."

"What are they?"

"I want you to check out James chapter 2 and especially verse 24. Study that and tell me what you think."

"What's the other verse?" I said.

"Well, the other one has to do with the purpose of baptism and it is Acts 2:38."

"Well, I'll tell you what, Cordell. I'll just borrow your Bible for now and if daddy says I can have it I'll be glad to have it. This Bible is almost new. It's a fine Bible. I thank you for letting me have it."

"I'll tell you what, Carl, I can't think of a better place for that Bible to be than in your hand. Take it with my blessing. Just read it."

I was happy to get that Bible. What a wonderful Bible it was. I was uneasy about what daddy would say about me having it because somebody gave it to me. Daddy would never take charity in any form. It was a great insult to him to think someone was giving him something out of pity. One time a lady at church gave me 3 shirts. She said her son had grew out of them and she wanted me to have them. That really made daddy mad. He would have no part of these shirts in our house. He made me take them back to her the next time I went to church. I wasn't sure what he would do about a Bible.

But for now I just couldn't wait to see what Cordell's verses had to say. What could possibly be in this Bible that he wanted me to read that was so important that he would give me an almost new Bible to get me to read it?

It was a long way down Montvale Road to the gravel road to my house. But as soon as I got to a clear place in the edge of the woods where I could sit down to read, I opened up the bible to read in James chapter 2 and starting in verse 19, I read:

James 2:19-24 (NKJV)
[19] You believe that there is one God. You do well. Even the demons believe--and tremble!

20 But do you want to know, O foolish man, that faith without works is dead?

21 Was not Abraham our father justified by works when he offered Isaac his son on the altar?

22 Do you see that faith was working together with his works, and by works faith was made perfect?

23 And the Scripture was fulfilled which says, "Abraham believed God, and it was accounted to him for righteousness." And he was called the friend of God.

24 You see then that a man is justified by works, and not by faith only.

"The demons believe and tremble." How could that be? If faith is all it takes to save us, then why would the demons not be saved? And why does it say that faith without works is dead? Reverend Milsaps said that the Bible says we are saved by faith only and nothing else. And yet, here in this Bible in James 2:24 it says that we are **not justified** by faith alone.

This was confusing. Why would the Bible contradict itself in this way?

What was the other verse he wanted me to look up? Let's see, it was Acts 2:38.

Acts 2:37-38 (NKJV)

37 Now when they heard this, they were cut to the heart, and said to Peter and the rest of the apostles, "Men and brethren, what shall we do?"

38 Then Peter said to them, "Repent, and let every one of you be baptized in the name of Jesus Christ for the remission of sins; and you shall receive the gift of the Holy Spirit.

"Baptized for the remission of sins?"

Could it be that Cordell was right? Surely that can't be.

Reverend Milsaps is a preacher of a church and Cordell is a barber. What could A barber know about the Bible. Cordell is not a man of God. There is no way he could know more about religion than Reverend Milsaps.

And still, everyone has told me that before I could be saved the Holy Spirit would have to come into my heart and allow me to understand what to do to be saved. And yet, here I read that Peter is saying that when we are baptized for the remission of our sins the Holy Spirit is given to us as a gift, afterwards.

What could all of this mean?

Could it be that the Bible contradicts itself? Why would all of these religious people read the Bible so different?

Some of the men at church are saying that all churches see the Bible different but it really doesn't matter anyway because we are all going to the same place in the end. I really didn't used to think that made much sense, but maybe they know more than I do about the Bible.

I closed the Bible and made my way home. I was more confused than ever. I had just began to get comfortable with the Baptist church and now Cordell's Bible made me start to look at things in a whole new suspicious way. And not just the Baptist church, but the Bible, too. Can the Bible be understood, I wondered?

At least one thing good happened with the gift of the Bible. For some reason, daddy didn't seem to object to me getting it as a gift. I told him that Cordell gave it to me and he looked at it and all he said was that it looked almost new. I may not be able to read it but at least it was mine to keep.

I hadn't told anyone about it and I don't think I even admitted it to myself, but I had always been a little bit afraid of mama's Bible. It was big and heavy and it was full of colored pictures of angels and devils and it even had a picture of Jesus hanging on the cross. It was hard for me to look at these pictures without thinking about heaven and hell and eternal fire and the earth being destroyed and what would all of that be like. Many times I would pick it up and think about maybe reading it but the very awesomeness of it all seemed too much for me to be comfortable with.

But this Bible from Cordell felt different. There were no pictures, and it could be that helped. And it was nowhere near as heavy as mama's. But that wasn't all. Cordell, or someone else, had underlined many of the passages in several places all through it. I found this to be somewhat like looking for treasure at times. I knew without being told that these passages were important to someone. Important enough that they marked them so that they would stand out and be easy to find. The passages Cordell had asked me to read were some of the ones that had been underlined.

I found this Bible interesting to read, at first. I knew I needed to read the Bible and I started out thinking that I would read the whole thing pretty quick. I had heard people's names called out at church, who had finished reading the whole Bible all the way through. Some of them had read it through more than once. So I started reading it myself. I started in the book of Genesis and I found it pretty interesting. I read through Genesis and Exodus and the Bible seemed to get harder to read. I didn't get much farther than that until I began to skip around and read sections at random. It wasn't long until I stopped altogether. It was a lot harder than I thought.

Chapter 6   I Joined the Church

The summer before I started the 8th grade was filled with newness in my life. I learned to swim, and that opened up a whole new world of adventure for me. Along with the ability to swim came a confidence with the river that opened up a complete new type of river fun. Edgar and I spent many summer nights camped out somewhere on the Little Calf River. I discovered the thrill of the canoe. Edgar was a "river rat." I could never have hoped to generate the confidence he had with a canoe. He was at home on the water. Just the very fact that he was so sure of himself and was so good at handling a canoe gave me courage to try anything he wanted to do. There were no rapids or falls on the river that we didn't at some point "run." There were times that I was literally terrified, but what great fun it was when it was all over.

I kissed a girl that summer.

It wasn't like I planned it. If I had planned it, I doubt that I would have been able to do it. In fact, it happened sort of spontaneously. Sometimes I wonder if I really did it at all, or did she kiss me?

It happened on a trip to Cade's Cove with the youth group from church. There was a bonfire after dark and we sat around the fire on logs and watched the sparks from the wood dance in the flames. The lightning bugs were flashing in the fields around the edge of the woods, and even for me it was really a mysterious moment in my life. I held hands with Anita and her eyes danced in the firelight. She was so beautiful. Strands of her hair fell across one eye in the night breeze and her smile was almost like it was directed especially for me and me alone. We held hands and we walked in the night not far away from the group but just enough to be in the darkness alone together.

We stopped and when she looked into my eyes and I held her close to me, neither one of us could have stopped the kiss that we shared together.

I don't know if she remembers it the same way I do, but it was a moment in my life that holds a place in my heart that could never be replaced.

These outings with the Victory Baptist church youth group were wonderful memories in my life. Being with this group brought a sense of peace to my life that otherwise would not have been there at all. I had a great fear of hell and the hereafter. Somehow this church and these other young people took that fear out of my mind.

On one of these outings, Reverend Milsaps went along with the group and he used this time to talk to me about joining the church. It went something like this.

"Carl, you've been baptized for quite some time now, have you been giving any thought to joining the church?"

"Joining the church? Well, no, I guess not. Is that something I need to do? I guess I just thought I was a member of Victory Baptist."

"Well, in one sense you are. You certainly are a part of the youth group. But you really need to make a decision about joining a church."

"Didn't I read somewhere in the Bible where God adds the people to the church that have been saved?" This was one of the passages in Cordell's Bible that I had found underlined. I remembered reading it but I had no idea where it was located. Looking back on it now I know that I was remembering Acts 2:47.

Acts 2:47 (NKJV)
> [47] *praising God and having favor with all the people. And the Lord added to the church daily those who were being saved.*

"Well, the Bible does say that, but that passage is just talking about the Christian being a part of the universal church in general. It's not talking about being a member of your local denomination."

"What would happen to me if I decided not to join a church, would I not be saved?"

"Oh no, nothing like that. You don't have to join a church if you don't want to. You can still go to heaven even if you never join any type of a formal church. Many people will be saved and never join any church. Or for that matter, you don't have to join the Baptist church to be saved. You can be saved in any denomination. But I still think a person should join some denomination."

"I hear people say that everyone should join the church of their choice. Does that include all the denominations?"

"Well, I wouldn't go quite that far. There are some out there that are just not Bible based churches. A person needs to stay away from them, but there are good people in almost all the denominations."

"Which one do you think I should join? I kind of thought I was a Baptist."

"Oh son, you are a Baptist. You've been here most of your life. You need to join The Victory Baptist Church."

"But that's really not the only reason you need to join the Baptist church. In reality, when you boil it all down, the Baptist church is the only one of the denominations that has it right. Most of the rest of the other denominations don't really understand what the Bible says about a lot of other things. The Baptist church has been around a lot longer than all the others and they have things that are really not proper Bible teaching."

"Are all these other denominations going to hell?"

"My goodness, no. They do things their way and we do things our way. All of us are going to the same place. It's really not so important to do everything just like the Bible says to do it as long as your heart is sincere in what you are trying to do. We may not be united in the things we teach but God is not impressed with legalists who want everything done just so. God is a God of love. He's impressed with our hearts and not what we do. He judges our hearts and our intent, and our works are like 'filthy rags' in the sight of God."

"What do I need to do to join the church?"

"Well, there's not much to it. I have a form letter in my office. I can fill it out for you and you'll need to have one of your parents sign it. When the church gets the letter asking for you to join the church, they'll vote on it and you will be appointed as a member."

Reverend Milsaps was as good as his word and the very next Sunday he gave me the letter and asked me to take it home and bring it back the next week.

I am not for sure why, but daddy refused to sign the letter. On the one hand that type of reaction was not so unusual for him, because there had been several things for school that he would not sign, either. But later on, I thought it might have been the things he learned growing up as a boy around relatives who were members of the Church of Christ.

But mama signed the letter, and I took it back.

It was several weeks before my name was announced on a Sunday morning and I became an official member of the Victory Baptist Church.

But many times over the next several months, I would turn to the underlined passage in Cordell's Bible and read where *"the Lord added to the church those who were being saved."*

Chapter 7   We Have To Move

It was a hot summer Saturday afternoon. I had helped daddy pick almost 2 bushels of ripe tomatoes and almost a bushel of Half Runner green beans. We always had a big garden and mama would can these green beans and turn these tomatoes into great tomato juice which she used for sauces and which I felt like I could almost drink my weight in it sometimes.

We had been working all morning and we had stopped for lunch and daddy had sat down on the chop block and lit up his pipe. The wood pile seemed to be daddy's favorite place to spend his time. If he was not sitting on the chop block, he was sawing slabs and poles into stove wood with his one man crosscut saw. We had a 2 man crosscut for the bigger logs and I put my share of time in with this thing as well. My brother Cliff was 8 years older than me and he could wear me out on the other end of a crosscut saw.

Today daddy had acted like he had something on his mind that was bothering him. He was quiet and had very little to say as we did our work together, and there was a couple of times when we stopped to rest and it seemed like he almost started to say something but then at the last minute he seemed to think better about it and nothing was said.

But now, at the chop block, he seemed to have picked up a little more confidence about telling me what he wanted me to know.

"Carl, there's something I wanted to talk to you about," he said.

"What's that?" I asked. Expecting him to say something about some kind of a plan he had for me to carry out some task while he was at work.

"Well, I don't know how to tell you this, son. But it looks like I've lost my job."

"Lost your job? You mean at the plant?" There was a horrified look on daddy's face when he saw how I reacted to his statement about the job. For just a minute it looked like he was about to cry. He quickly recovered and corrected that emotion that was totally out of place for him. Daddy was not one to show an emotion that would make him look weak in someone else's eyes. If he had ever thought that I saw this emotion in his face he would have been mortified beyond belief. I knew how he felt about that and I would never have hurt him by saying anything about it. But I was shocked and he could see it in my face.

"Does mama know about it?" I asked.

"Yeah, she knows. I've been seeing it coming for weeks. It looks like Alcoa is shutting down the farm and they'll just stick to making aluminum."

"What are you going to do?" I asked.

"Well, I put in my application at the plant to work inside. I don't know. They told me at the office that they had doubts about hiring anybody with a 4th grade education."

"That doesn't seem fair. You've been there ever since I was a baby. Don't that count for something?"

"Well it might. They haven't told me anything yet. But it doesn't really look good."

"But this is what I need to tell you, son. It looks like there won't be any income for a while unless I can get some odd jobs or something. It looks like we may have to tighten our belts 'till we see how this goes."

"Is there anything I can do?"

"No, we'll make out somehow. We have enough canned goods to last us for quite a while. You can help cut hay and fodder for the stock."

"What about Cliff? Can he donate whatever he makes from Maude Presley?" Cliff was working on Maude Presley's dairy farm as a hired hand.

"He'll help some, but he's planning on getting married in a few months. I just can't take all he makes away from him."

"But we'll make it somehow. We'll take each day as it comes and we'll make it."

Daddy seemed to have confidence in our ability to make it without the job on Alcoa Aluminum Company's farm and that was comforting to me. Daddy had grown up in a time when hardly anyone worked at a public job. His daddy certainly didn't. He made a living and supported his family by farming and living off the mountain. I guess daddy thought he could do the same.

But that was not to be so.

A few weeks went by and it actually seemed to me that things were better than they were when daddy worked. He was home every day and our fields and crops never looked so good. We would cut tobacco in a week or two and there was not a weed in our fields. But that changed.

We rented our house from an old man named Wendell Blair. Daddy was sitting on the wood pile one evening and Mr. Blair drove into our yard and walked over to the wood pile where daddy was sitting. The two of them talked for a few minutes and daddy's head seemed to drop, just for a moment, and he recovered again and stood up off the wood pile and they spoke for just another minute or two and Mr. Blair got in his car and dust boiled up as he drove on down Pea Ridge Road toward Frank Hall's store.

Daddy sat for a few more minutes on the wood pile and he got up and slowly made his way up on the back porch where mama was standing with her hands in her apron pockets. I made my way around the house and came up on the other side of the house, out of sight of the view from the back porch.

"What did he say?" Mama asked.

"Well, he wants his rent." daddy replied.

"Did you tell him you are out of work?" she asked.

"Yeah, he knows. We're 2 months behind and he says I just need to pay up what we owe."

"What did you tell him you would do?" mama asked.

"I offered him the crops and the tobacco crop for the rent, but he said he couldn't settle for that. He said he had a share of the crops anyway and he just wants cash for the rent."

"What kind of a man is he?" mama said. "Our part of the tobacco crop should be worth 3 or 4 month's rent."

"Well, I guess you can't blame him for wanting his rent money. I just wish he would give us just a little more time."

"How much time do we have?" mama asked. I heard a sob in her voice as she said it.

"We have 30 days," daddy said. "We have to be out in 30 days."

At this point mama could hold it no more and she burst into tears. Like many Appalachian women it was not like her to cry. At this, I stepped from the side of the house and mama saw me. She threw her apron over her head and ran back into the house in tears.

Daddy said, "I guess you heard?"

"I heard," I said. Nothing else was said by either of us and daddy walked back to the wood pile and lit his pipe and sat there looking off at the mountain about 5 miles away.

A few days went by and not much more was said to me about what we were going to do. Finally, I could stand it no longer and I asked daddy if he had any idea where we were going to move.

"Well it looks like we'll move out with your aunt Velma for a while. I asked her about that shed Birch built when they were first building their house. They lived in it for a while with 2 kids. I thought we could maybe stay there 'till things get settled."

"You mean the place where they have all that junk stored? When we were out there a few months ago they had chickens in there."

"Well, we'll clean it up. It'll work for a while 'till we can do better. Say, I'm going to have to go to the store after awhile. You can go with me if you want to."

We didn't buy groceries at Frank Hall's grocery store. Our regular trading was done with Huff and McMurray's Store on Montvale Road. It was a pretty good walk to get there but we were used to it and sometimes our groceries would be delivered and we could ride the delivery truck back home. Almost all grocery stores had free delivery in those days.

Huff and McMurray's store was what would have been the local super market in those days. It was a small place and had limited supplies but it was the local shopping place for most of the people in the community without cars.

I followed daddy through the aisles of the store and he picked up some common staples we used almost every day. I remember a 4 pound bucket of lard for one thing and some JFG coffee for another. All in all he had several items and we made our way to the counter. There were several people in the small one room store and 2 or 3 were sitting around a checker board playing checkers.

Mr. McMurray rang up the groceries and some of the men were talking to daddy while we stood at the counter.

"That will be $5.60, Cooper," Mr. McMurray said.

"Can you just put that on my bill?" daddy said.

"Did you know your bill is past due?" Mr. McMurray said.

This was mortifying to my daddy. I could see it in his face. Mr. McMurray had made no effort to lower his voice and he had said these things to daddy in front of all of the people in the store.

I never had any use for this man or this store after that. That was the last time I ever set foot in that store until almost 40 years later. I saw, one time many years later, that the store had been turned into an art gallery and I went in to look around. There was an old Huff and McMurray calendar hanging on the wall. I mentioned the calendar to the people who worked in the art gallery and not one person remembered who Huff and McMurray were. Somehow that pleased me.

Daddy looked at Mr. McMurray and stood, stunned for just a minute, and he reached in to his pocket and lay what change he had in his pocket on the counter and it came to $1.65.

"Will that be enough to get the lard?", daddy said.

One of the men in the store saw what was happening to daddy and stepped up to the counter and told daddy that he would loan him the money to get it all if he wanted to.

I knew that daddy would never accept charity from anybody. There was no way he would take money from someone to pay a bill and buy groceries for him. Many people could have taken it but this would have the ultimate damaged to his pride; more than he would have been able to bear.

Mr. McMurray rang up the bucket of lard and took the $1.65 and we walked out of the store and headed home.

"Don't tell your mama about this," he said.

Mama cleaned up the shack at Aunt Velma's. Velma was daddy's sister and I liked her. Unlike daddy, she was a talker. She and mama got along fine and she pitched in and helped and the shack actually looked somewhat livable when they got through.

We moved in at the end of summer.

We left our crops and we left the tobacco for Blair to do with as he thought fit. It was worth more than the rent and so we considered the matter paid in full. I never saw the Blair's again after that day.

That wasn't all I missed. Moving was especially hard for me. I never went back to Victory Baptist Church and I never saw Edgar or Anita again. And for a long time I grieved for these memories. But events changed for me and new friends, new adventures, and a new church were the results. I was on the threshold of the destiny of a new life, but at this moment in time I had no way to know it.

Chapter 8   Aunt Velma's Church

Daddy gave Uncle Birch the mule and the animals we had. Birch didn't want any pay to live in his shed, but nothing would do other than he take the stock. We kept the chickens and one pig and we slaughtered all of them over the course of the next few weeks. I had no way of knowing it at the time but this was the last farming our family would ever do. Our lives had already changed and nothing would ever be the same again.

I can't remember just how long we lived in the shed before me and mama accompanied Aunt Velma to church. It wasn't very long. Aunt Velma was a member of the Wildwood Church of Christ. Uncle Birch was like daddy, he never went to church but he would always drive Velma and then come back and pick her up after church was over.

The first thing I noticed about the Wildwood Church of Christ was that the building was small. And not only was it small, but it really didn't even look like a church building to me. There was no steeple, I could see that right off and the windows looked more like windows in a house rather than a church. The windows in the Victory Baptist church were huge and made out of all colors of glass. I noticed that there were no bells ringing like I was used to at Victory Baptist. Everything about the building seemed to be more like a house than a church. I wasn't very impressed with Aunt Velma's church from the outside.

The inside of the church was pretty plain as well. There was a podium on a raised stage of sorts in the front and I took it that that must be where the preacher stands to preach. But the inside lacked any majestic art work and colored paintings on the wall like I was used to, and there was no place that I could see for the choir to sit for the music. And not only that, there was no organ or piano anywhere to be seen.

The pews were not too bad. They had no padding and were just plain wood but the wood grain was pretty. In the back of each pew were song books and Bibles and every so often there was a hand held fan with the picture of a funeral home in pretty colors. All in all it was a plain building but it was neat and clean and arranged to look presentable. It certainly didn't intimidate me I could say that. I was always intimidated and frightened to a degree with just the building alone at the Victory Baptist Church, not to mention the bells and organ music and the way the preacher's voice rose and fell and the deep breaths he would take between words as he preached.

There were not very many people at church here today. Not like the crowd I was used to for a Sunday morning. There were probably not more than 60 people in all, if that many. And I didn't see very many young people my age. I saw about 3 or 4 that looked like they may be in high school and there were a few others who were younger than me and looked to be in lower grades. There was 1 boy and 1 girl who seemed about my age as best I could tell. I wasn't very impressed with Aunt Velma's church.

The worship service was simple enough. We started out with a song leader in the front of the assembly and he led 2 or 3 songs and the congregation all sang together. There was no organ but I figured that a church no bigger than this could not afford to own one and so they did without. And then they had communion. I had seen communion served at Victory Baptist and this was not such a surprise other than I was amazed that I just happened to show up on this one day when communion would be observed.

But it was the preacher that was so different. More so

than any preacher I had ever heard in my all life. Aunt Velma said the preacher's name was Brother Scarbrough. The first thing I noticed about the way he preached was the way he spoke to the church. His voice was just like any other person giving a talk to a group. It didn't seem to me like he was preaching at all. He was talking to the crowd. This was the first time I had ever heard a preacher talk like this.

But what really surprised me was the sermon he had prepared. I had never heard anything like it. He talked about an "Original Church" and he told us that this "Original Church" preached the "Original Gospel". This was strange to me and it certainly got my attention. And then he told us that this original Gospel was the only Gospel that God recognized as being approved as truth. He said that this was the same Gospel that Paul preached and it is the same Gospel that should be preached today. He used a Scripture that would eventually be very important to me when the day would come that I would understand more about what he was telling us about the church and the Gospel of Christ. It was:

Galatians 1:6-9 (NKJV)
⁶ I marvel that you are turning away so soon from Him who called you in the grace of Christ, to a different gospel,
⁷ which is not another; but there are some who trouble you and want to pervert the gospel of Christ.
⁸ But even if we, or an angel from heaven, preach any other gospel to you than what we have preached to you, let him be accursed.
⁹ As we have said before, so now I say again, if anyone preaches any other gospel to you than what you have received, let him be accursed.

Brother Scarbrough told us that the Apostle Paul had preached the Gospel to the people of Galatia and it was only a short time until people started trying to change the message of salvation to suit themselves. He said that this very thing has been going on from that time until this very day. No wonder there are so many denominations and religions in the world today. Men have changed the teachings of the Gospel and the doctrines of the Church to please themselves and ignored the "Original Gospel" that was given to us by the Bible and the Apostle Paul. And here in these passages in *Galatians 1* Paul tells us not to alter or change this teaching even if we are told to do so by an angel from Heaven.

The reason this was so interesting to me and the reason it captivated me so much was because Reverend Milsaps had told me specifically that all churches and denominations were approved by God. Does this Brother Scarbrough really know what he is talking about? How could some preacher in a little old place like this know more than reverend Milsaps? I would think, not very likely.

But that wasn't all he had to say about "one Gospel."

He had us look in our Bibles to another passage in John 17.

John 17:20-21 (NKJV)
20 *"I do not pray for these alone, but also for those who will*
  believe in Me through their word;
21 *that they all may be one, as You, Father, are in Me, and I in*
  You; that they also may be one in Us, that the world may
  believe that You sent Me.

The minute I turned to these passages in John 17, I saw that these very passages were underlined in Cordell's Bible. I had brought the Bible with me and somehow, this seemed to make these passages more mysterious to me and make me want to know more about what they had to say.

Brother Scarbrough had studied these passages, it was plain to see, and he explained it like this:

This was a prayer by Jesus on the very night He was betrayed. He knew He was about to die on the cross and he prayed for His disciples and for all people that would be influenced to have faith through their words. Jesus' dying request was for all of his disciples and followers to be united as "one." He wants all of us, even today, to be "one" as He and God are "one."

This means that Jesus expects us to teach the same doctrines, to be united in the church, and not to break up into denominations and teach different things and different "Gospels".

This might be a small church building and this place may not be intimidating and awesome, but this makes more sense than anything I've ever heard inside a church. I was impressed with the logic of the sermon I had just heard. And not only that, everything he said, I was able to read in Cordell's Bible. And if that wasn't enough, all of the passages he referred to were underlined by someone who had read these passages before. I can see why someone would underline these passages. If this was important enough for Jesus to pray about as a last request before He died, it must be important enough for us to know about today.

I left Aunt Velma's church a little more impressed than when I first arrived. I told Aunt Velma that I would like to hear this man again and hear more of what he had to say. Little did I know as we left the church that I would never hear Brother Scarbrough again. It would be years before I ever returned to this church and by then Brother Scarbrough had moved on.

Chapter 9   A lucky Break

I started Porter School in the 8th grade. I had no choice in the matter. I had to go to school and this was where I was assigned to go. I was not comfortable to go there. I was so out of place in that school. Porter was a much more modern building than Forest Hill Elementary and I was like a fish out of water. I didn't know anyone in that school and by the end of the first day; even I could see that there was something wrong with my clothes. Wide legged overall jeans and an outing shirt was out of place in a school where the kids had western jeans and poodle skirts.

Uncle Birch and Aunt Velma's place still looked like a working farm but the community of Wildwood was changing fast. Most of the people worked for Alcoa Aluminum Company and farms were being abandoned for a more modern and easy type of life. Even Uncle Birch worked for the Aluminum Company now. He worked at the plant we called the pot rooms. Aluminum was melted down into aluminum ingots and sent to the roller mill to be turned into aluminum foil and other aluminum products.

I settled down after a couple of weeks at Porter School. I was a pretty good student and I made good grades. School was easy for me and most of the time I liked school. The school had rules, and I liked that. Rules always seemed to give order to everything and they let you know what you needed to do. I was always good at following rules. That is, as long as they made sense to me.

I had hardly gotten started at Porter School and began to be a little more at ease in this strange environment when daddy got notice from the plant that he was being hired to work inside. Mama was overjoyed with this news and I feel sure that she had visions of returning to a life on the farm like she had lived all her life. Mama was a simple woman. She had no formal education and she had gone through the 3rd or 4th grade in school. She was comfortable on the farm and it was something she could do well. But little did she know that she was destined never to return. In fact, none of us would.

Daddy got the job and although the pay was not great, it was almost twice what he made working on the Aluminum Company farm. This was more money than daddy had ever made. Looking back, I am not sure if this was a blessing for our family or a curse. Mama was out of place with populated community living and she never learned to "fit in" to that type of environment and life. She was backward and shy around people that she didn't know and she tried her best to avoid people as best she could.

Daddy found us another place to live.

It wasn't really much but it was a tremendous upgrade for all of us. There was water inside the house. Well, sort of. We had a kitchen sink and there was a faucet with a spigot running into that sink. There were no bathrooms in the house and no showers or tubs, and we still had an outdoor toilet, but it was closer to the house. We had neighbors on each side of us and across the street and all around us. What a thrill this was for me. I had never lived this close to people before in all my life. The community of Bungalow was like living in a small town. I learned to love this community. There were many young people my age and in a very short time I was surrounded with friends and companions. It wasn't very long until I knew almost every family in the community.

There was no more farming for our family after that. The daily chores that I had been used to had been reduced to almost none. I had plenty of time for exploring the woods and the fields and the creeks and all the wonderful adventures that a young boy could dream up. While I lived at Bungalow and the entire time I attended the 8th grade, church took a back seat in my life.

We only lived in the community of Bungalow for about a year. And as much as I loved this community, it was better, as it turned out that we moved. In fact, it just may have been the providence of God to place me into an environment where I encountered friends who helped me to learn things about the Bible and the church that I would otherwise never have heard.

Daddy wanted us to have a better life and that would include a house with a bathroom and showers and more modern conveniences than we had at Bungalow. We moved to another community almost like Bungalow called Eagleton Village. This move was not as disruptive to me as the others were. Eagleton Village was almost like Bungalow. It was filled with kids my own age and it was a simple step to find numerous friends. But by now, I was ready to enter high school and it meant attending Everett High. I had heard about this school all my life. My brother Cliff had attended there and so had every one I knew who had lived in our county for very long. This high school served the entire county and I couldn't wait to go myself. The kids from Eagleton Village would attend there and so would the friends I knew from Bungalow. Some of my friends had driver's licenses and would occasionally be able to get their family car and pick me up. This was a wonderful time in my life and I have fond memories of these days at Everett High.

Whether God set this up or not, I may never know. But as luck would have it, we moved into a house next door to a family who were members of the Church of Christ.

The Tipton's were a great family. There were 4 kids and they were all around my age. The oldest was a girl who was about 2 years older than me and there were 2 girls younger than me.

And then there was Rex. He was my age, and we became great friends.

My first day at Everett High was wonderful. There were so many people that I knew that it was almost like I had been there all along. Some things were handled different with the way the school days were structured and designed. I was not used to changing classrooms every hour to attend a different class and I was not used to study halls and homeroom. But on my first day at school, there was an assembly called, for all the freshmen. I remember very little about that orientation speech but I remember the skit the seniors put on for us. The girls all sang and danced and some of them wore grass skirts. Suddenly, without warning, in the middle of the performance, here comes one of the senior boys across the stage with a lawn mower. This was hilarious. I knew for sure that I was going to like high school. And I did.

The Everett campus was a big place. There were at least 5 buildings with an auditorium and a gymnasium. There was a football field with a track around it and I seemed to have classes at some point in about all of them. Across the street was a snack bar where many of the kids ate lunch. Sometimes I would go over there myself. Many of the kids said that they hated the lunchroom food. Not me, I loved the lunchroom food. Mama was a simple country woman and she had no exotic recipes like the lunchroom served. I liked the things the lunchroom served. But the snack bar was a place to meet friends and to hang out during lunch.

I had been to Everett almost 2 months when I encountered something I never expected to happen. I decided to go to the snack bar today instead of the lunch room and when I walked in I saw Linda Tipton sitting at a booth with a boy. Linda was 1 grade ahead of me and she was a sophomore. Linda was sitting with a boy with his back turned to me. When Linda saw me come in, she called out, "Carl, come and sit with us." The place was crowded as usual and there was an empty seat in the booth with her. I made my way to the booth and sat down. I looked at the boy across from Linda on the other side of the booth and I couldn't believe my eyes.

"Jay Thomas?" I said.

"Carl Cooper?" he said.

"Jay Thomas told me he knew you," Linda said.

"Are you kidding, we grew up together at Forest Hill. I had no idea he was at Everett. How are you? Where do you live at? I didn't even know you were alive. The last time I saw you, you were pretty sick."

"Yeah, I had polio. I almost died. I'm over it now. I have a slight limp because I wear a brace on one leg, but otherwise, I survived it."

"You wear a brace?"

"Yeah, I wear a brace but I manage pretty well. I limp a little but it doesn't slow me down. I can drive a car."

"You have your license? I thought we were the same age. Are you a freshman?"

"No, I'm a sophomore. I missed school when my daddy died and I was behind at Forest Hill. I made it up while I was sick and I skipped a grade. I'm caught up now."

"How's your mama? Is she doing OK?"

"Well, mama remarried. She married a man she met where she works. She got a job at the Standard Knitting Mill. We had it pretty tough there for a long time while I was sick. We had to move from Forest Hill, you know. Mama got some help from the March of Dimes people and they moved us into a place over in

Maryville. When I got better, mama got a job with Standard Knitting and she's been there ever since."

"She married James Best while she worked there. James works for Alcoa Aluminum now."

"Did you say you can drive?"

"Yeah, I can drive. I have my license. That is, I can drive when James will let me borrow the car."

"Linda has her license, too. She drives sometimes."

"Yeah, I know Linda. I know the whole Tipton family. I know Rex and all their sisters and Mrs. Tipton."

"How do you know the Tipton's? They live right next door to me."

"Do you live in Eagleton Village? I thought you lived at Forest Hill."

"No. we had to move from Forest Hill. Not long after you took sick, daddy lost his job at the Alcoa Farm and he was out of a job. We had to move out from Blair's place."

"Does he have a job now?"

"Yeah, he works at the plant. How did you say you know the Tiptons?"

"I go to church with them."

"You go to church with them?"

"Yep."

"You know, I haven't been to church in a long time. I used to go to Victory Baptist where you and I used to go, but I haven't been in a long while."

"You can always go with me," Linda said.

"You ought to come with her," Jay Thomas said.

"Maybe I will. Are you there all the time?"

"I never miss if there is any way I can get there. Mama and James go there and so I always have a ride. And that's not all, Carl.

"I've learned a lot about the church and about the Bible since I started there. I help to teach the high school Bible class now. I remember the questions you used to ask at Victory Baptist. I used to ask the same questions you did. I know a lot of the answers now. You and I need to get together pretty soon."

We had sat there so long that we ran out of time to order anything to eat. I didn't care. This was a wonderful surprise to find my friend Jay Thomas alive and well and attending the same school I was. We said our goodbyes and promised to see each other again as soon as we could. I told Jay Thomas that I would try to come to church with the Tiptons the next time they came.

I never had any idea that I would ever see Jay Thomas again. I thought that he must be dead. And yet, here he was, alive and in the same school I was once again.

In later years I decided that this, too, must have been the providence of God. The effect this meeting would have on the rest of my life was way more than I could ever have even imagined at this point in my life. But I know now that he did more for me to help me develop as a Christian than anyone else in my life.

Chapter 10   **Hard Questions**

For the next few weeks I avoided going to church with Linda and Rex. It had been quite a while since I had been to church and to tell you the truth, I really wasn't sure what I needed to do about going to church. I used to consider myself a Baptist and I was supposed to be a member of Victory Baptist Church, but I had not been back there since we moved from Forest Hill. What was I now, I wondered? And for that matter, does it really matter anyway? Reverend Milsaps had told me that the Baptist Church was the church that "had Bible teaching right", but I sure was impressed with what I heard from Aunt Velma's preacher, Brother Scarbrough. You might say that I was a little bit confused about some of the teaching about the Bible I was hearing.

But that didn't stop me from renewing my friendship with Jay Thomas. The Tipton's had 2 cars since Mr. and Mrs. Tipton both worked and both drove a car to work. Linda had her license and she had access to a car just about all the time. This was a definite convenience to me. Linda was always ready to take me and Rex for a ride as long as we could pick up Jay Thomas to go with us. We could spend hours sitting parked at Richy Kreme or Creamland drive in hamburger joints, sipping on Cokes and talking and having fun. Sometimes we would drive the 5 miles between the two restaurants and just circle the parking lot, wave at our high school friends and head back to the other. What great fun this was during this special time in my life.

It was on one of these special nights while we were sitting in the curb service parking lot at Richy Kreme hamburger shop that the subject of baptism came up.

Jay Thomas said, "Carl, have you been baptized?"

"Sure," I said. "I was baptized in the Maryville College swimming pool by Reverend Milsaps from the Victory Baptist Church."

"Why were you baptized?" Jay Thomas said.

"Why? Well, I can't really tell you why, exactly. But after I was saved, Reverend Milsaps told me that I needed to be baptized, and I was. But, to tell you the truth, several people have asked me the same question and here you are asking me why I was baptized, too. I've had people tell me that I'm not really saved because I was baptized for the wrong reason. I'm not really sure why I was baptized, but I do know that I was saved."

"How do you know you were saved? Did someone tell you that you were saved or did you read it in the Bible?"

"Well, now that you mention it, I'm not sure I remember exactly how I knew it. Looking back on it, I guess it just sort of came in stages as I went to church. I know I was told that I needed to be saved in order to go to Heaven. I think I must have known that even before I started going to church."

"Well, let me ask you this," Jay Thomas said. "Suppose I were to ask you what I needed to do in order to be saved. What would you tell me to do?"

"Well that's a new twist," I said. "It's always been the other way around. I've never had anybody ask me what they need to do. I've always been the one asking what I need to do."

"So, what would you tell me to do?" Jay Thomas said.

"I'm not sure I should be trying to answer a question like that," I said. "Don't you think we should leave questions about religious things like that to preachers and pastors and people who specialize in religious things?"

These words had barely left my lips when I could see what looked like a surprised expression on Jay Thomas' face.

"Carl, do you read the Bible very much?" he asked.

"Not as much as I should, I guess," I said. "Why?"

"Well, do you believe the Bible is the true Word of God?"

"Sure I do. The Bible is God's Holy Word."

"Well if the Bible is God's Holy Word to all of us then what should we do if we read something in the Bible? Should we do what the Bible tells us to do or would we be free to just ignore it and do it our way instead?"

"I don't think there's any question about that." I said. "We should do anything the Bible tells us to do. If God tells someone to do something, then we should do it."

"Are you sure you feel that way?" Jay Thomas said. "Many people say they believe that, but when the chips are down and it becomes inconvenient, they change their mind."

"Not me," I said. "Why would anyone not want to do something if the Bible tells them to do it?"

"Trust me," Jay Thomas said. "The world is filled with people who twist the Scriptures to try to get the words to say what they want them to mean. Lots of people just don't want to do what the Bible tells them to do. They go to great lengths to try to make the Bible say something in a way that agrees with how they want things to be."

"Now that you mention it, I've heard a lot of different opinions about church things lately."

"Well, let me ask you that question, what must I do to be saved, again. You said you thought a pastor or preacher should be the only type people who should answer these types of questions. But what would you do if the Bible told you that you needed to be the one to answer them?"

"Does the Bible say that?"

"Yep, it sure does. Rex, is there a Bible in the back seat?"

"Carl, read what the Bible says in 1 Peter 3:15."

I read these verses:

1 Peter 3:15 (NKJV)

> *But sanctify the Lord God in your hearts, and always be ready to give a defense to everyone who asks you a reason for the hope that is in you, with meekness and fear;*

"Is that talking about me?" I asked. "Does God expect me to always be ready to teach every person who asks me how to be saved? I can't really do that."

"God tells us here to get ready to be able to do it." Jay Thomas said. "Do you still think you should do everything the Bible tells you to do?"

"This is hard, Jay Thomas. I really can't do that. I don't really know enough about the Bible to do it."

"Well that's true right now. But God will give you time to learn. This verse is telling you to become ready. You may not be completely ready right now, but you can get ready. Of course you can't get ready unless you start studying your Bible."

"You know, Jay Thomas, I've tried reading the Bible and it's not as easy to understand as people would lead you to think."

"You're right, Carl. God designed a special way for people to learn about the Gospel. In the beginning when someone starts out trying to understand the Scriptures, they need a teacher. And not just any teacher. There are many false teachers out there teaching error. In fact, there are many times more false teachers than there are those who understand the Bible truths. The Bible calls these teachers wolves in sheep's clothing."

"How will I know the difference?" I said.

"Simple, you must follow along in your own Bible and read for yourself what the Bible has to say. Don't just take someone's word for something just because they appear to be religious. You've got to be able to read it and understand it for yourself. If you can't do that, it may not be truth at all."

"Read what the Bible says in Romans 10:14:

Romans 10:14 (NKJV)

> *How then shall they call on Him in whom they have not believed? And how shall they believe in Him of whom they have not heard? And how shall they hear without a preacher?*

"You can substitute the word 'Teacher' for the word 'Preacher' and it applies the same way here. When a person starts out trying to study the Scriptures they need a teacher. After they understand the basic divisions and doctrines, they then become the teacher themselves.

"Look at this verse in Acts 8:30. This is the story about the Ethiopian Eunuch. The Eunuch said he could not understand what he was reading unless someone guided him. He was a devout man and he studied the Scriptures, but he still needed a teacher."

Acts 8:30-31 (NKJV)

> *So Philip ran to him, and heard him reading the prophet Isaiah, and said, "Do you understand what you are reading?" And he said, "How can I, unless someone guides me?" And he asked Philip to come up and sit with him.*

"Wow, this is complicated," I said. "I think I need a teacher."

"You couldn't get a better teacher than Jay Thomas," Linda said. "He's the assistant teacher for the high school class at church."

"But will he teach me?" I said.

"Don't worry, Carl. We'll learn the Bible together. I'm not through learning myself. We'll teach each other."

And so it began for me. The next 3 years were some of the greatest memories of my life. Jay Thomas and Linda and Rex were the greatest of friends. Jay Thomas was as good as his word. We studied together and we had fun together. What great adventures we shared together as we grew up in that simple time period in East Tennessee.

And yet on this day in my life I could not answer the question, *"What must I do to be saved?"*

Chapter 11　　**The Bible Class**

After my discussion with Jay Thomas about studying the Bible, I made up my mind to try out the Tipton's church. My first opportunity came the following Wednesday night. Sure enough, Rex asked me to ride with them to church. Mr. Tipton did not attend church. He was a good man in every way. He was a good husband and father and he was a good friend to me, but he did not go with his family to church. This never changed until the day my daddy died. When my daddy died with a massive stroke, Mr. Tipton changed his life. From that day on he never missed a service at church and was faithful to attend for the rest of his life. But at this time, Mrs. Tipton drove the car and there were her 4 kids and me as passengers. It was crowded, to say the least but she never complained.

Wednesday night service consisted of Bible classes for all age groups. I went with Linda and Rex to the high school class. I was overjoyed to find Jay Thomas in the class as the assistant teacher. Jay Thomas had very little to do with the actual teaching of the class but was somewhat of a helper for the teacher in keeping the roll and reading Scriptures and anything the teacher asked him to do. I felt sure that Jay Thomas could have handled the class had he been called on to do so.

The teacher's name was Robert Hall. He looked like he might have been about 40 years old. He was well prepared for teaching the class and I could tell he knew his Bible material. And unlike any Bible class I had ever attended, there were no quarterlies. Robert Hall taught the class using the Bible alone for his book. Strange, I thought to myself.

But in spite of the strangeness of the class, this was one of the most interesting classes I had ever attended. The subject was the Old Testament characters, Nadab and Abihu in Leviticus Chapter 10;

Leviticus 10:1-2 (NKJV)

> *Then Nadab and Abihu, the sons of Aaron, each took his censer and put fire in it, put incense on it, and offered profane fire before the Lord, which He had not commanded them. So fire went out from the Lord and devoured them, and they died before the Lord.*

What a great story this was and what a great truth was being taught here that applied to all ages down through history and even today.

Robert Hall asked this question to the class.

What did Nadab and Abihu do wrong?

As you read this story for the first time you might decide that they didn't do very much wrong at all. They were Priests. In fact they were the sons of the High Priest, Aaron, the brother of Moses. Their job was to put fire in their censors from the alter. We don't know where the fire came from which they used, but the Bible calls it "strange fire". Wherever they got the fire it was not done as God had instructed them to do it. They decided to alter God's worship to suit themselves. They did it their own way and did not obey God's instructions. They "helped God out" by redesigning God's pattern of worship which He designed Himself.

Now at first this seems like such a simple thing to be killed for. Men have been doing this for thousands of years. Look at all of the types of worship that people have designed to present to God down through the years and even exist today. Doesn't it seem like fire is fire and not so much to be concerned about? Most people tend to think this same way. Most people just say "worship is worship" why make such a big deal about the form we present to God. Why wouldn't God just accept all forms of worship as the same?

But the problem here is obedience.

God is concerned with obedience in everything we do. When God tells us to do something in a certain way, then we are to obey the instructions we are given. The story of Nadab and Abihu tells us that God is serious about obedience to what He tells us to do. We are not to redesign God's plans and present to Him "strange fire" because we like it our way better. It doesn't matter how sincere our motives are, God is serious about our obedience to His instructions.

There is another passage found in Hebrews 5:10 that tells us that obedience is required for us to have salvation and eternal life.

Hebrews 5:8-9 (NKJV)
> though He was a Son, yet He learned obedience by the things which He suffered. And having been perfected, He became the author of eternal salvation to all who obey Him,

Now as you can see by reading this passage, obedience is not merely suggested but it is required in order to have eternal salvation.

When I read these passages it called to mind what Jay Thomas asked me a few days ago when he asked if I thought I needed to obey any instructions I found written in the Bible. Even then, I answered yes to that question.

But I could see by reading this Scripture that I needed more Bible study. How could people think that God would "just overlook" redesigning all the religious things people do in their churches? Where in the world did all these ideas come from and how did they start?

Reverend Milsaps had told me that not many churches see the Bible alike but yet all were approved by God. I wonder if Reverend Milsaps has considered Nadab and Abihu.

The class was over and I was deep in thought. I sat there while the class dismissed and I heard a voice calling my name.

"Carl," It was Jay Thomas' voice. "Let's go for a ride. I've got mama's car until midnight. We need a dollar for gas."

I had a quarter and Jay Thomas had a quarter, We quickly found Linda and Rex and they had 75 cents. This gave us $1.25 worth of Spur gas at 20 cents per gallon. This was enough to get us around Creamland and Richy Kreme and maybe even out to the skating rink and back. We took off.

Now Jay Thomas did have a driver's license. And I don't think his weak leg was really a handicap that hindered his driving ability. But I wouldn't say he was considered a good driver. We sat at Richy Kreme for a long time and it started to rain heavy. As we left Richy Kreme and started back up through Maryville the brakes started to make a terrible screeching noise on Jay Thomas' mother's car and the wheels begin to grab and slide every time we came to a stop light. It seemed like every stop light in town was destined to make us stop. Jay Thomas thought this was great fun and he turned it into a great joke. The more we became embarrassed with what was going on, the funnier he though the whole thing was. That's when we spotted the cop setting at the next light. Jay Thomas knew the car would make the screeching noise and slide the wheels if the red light caught us so he gunned the car to try to get through the light and you can guess what happened next. The red light got him and he hit the brakes. The wheels locked up with a great slide. We were all over the wet road. Jay Thomas wanted to send a signal to the cop to tell him that it was the fault of the car and not just bad driving on his part and so he put both feet up into the windshield of the car on the dash for the cop to see.

Now you would think this was a clear signal that anyone would appreciate and understand. And not only that, it was hilariously funny to everyone in the car. But for some reason the cop didn't see it nearly as funny as the rest of us did. Jay Thomas was raked over the coals by the cop and he didn't think much of the rest of us either. I'm pretty sure he thought he had stumbled onto a nest of juvenile delinquents and he was bound and determined to throw the book at all of us and run us out of town for the safety of all the honest town folks that we might corrupt. Naturally the car was impounded and Jay Thomas' mother was called to come and get us. No one got a ticket, thank goodness. I think it was only because the cop could not think of a category to write the ticket under.

This was just one of the times Jay Thomas' driving got us into trouble. Maryville was built on a hill like many towns are. Once we were coming down one of the hills coming out of town and Jay Thomas was just too fast for the curves and we knocked a mailbox off the post and sent it hurling through some man's yard. Jay Thomas was one of the smartest boys I ever knew. He had a full scholarship to go to the University of Tennessee all paid for him, but he was hard on his mama's cars. He once referred to himself as a "wreck less kid" but that changed when he hit the hay wagon on Hwy. 411 going home from church.

I never saw Linda Tipton as a girlfriend. But she had a friend named Joyce Harviston who sometimes came to visit her. I was invited to go on a hay ride with Linda and Joyce. I guess I was supposed to be Joyce's date for the hay ride. We sat together under the blanket and whispered to each other and held hands. There were several kisses in the moonlight and in the dark.

And like the night with Anita at Victory Baptist Church this night holds memories that I never forgot. I often wonder if she remembers them too.

I saw Joyce several times after that when she would come to visit the Tipton's. But these visits stopped and I was told that Joyce's family had moved to Nashville. I never saw or heard from her after that. Linda told me several years later that Joyce had married a man in Nashville and had 2 kids.

The Tipton's had a big front porch on their house. Now their house was not big. It was like all the other houses in Eagleton Village, but their house had a front porch that was as long as the house. It was not at all unusual for Mrs. Tipton to invite the youth group from church to their house for fun and food and I was always there. I lived next door so I was a major part of the fun and food. One night as I sat on the front porch at one of these meetings Jay Thomas asked me if I had given any more thought as to telling him what I thought he needed to do in order to be saved. I had been thinking about that and I had been listening to what was being said at church.

"I've been meaning to talk to you about that." I said.

"When I was in the Baptist church I was told that the only thing a person needed to be saved was faith alone. If a person has faith that Jesus is God's Son then that's all that's required to be saved. But even with that I was still told that I needed to say the sinner's prayer and ask Jesus to come into my heart to be saved."

"So, is that what you would tell me to do to be saved?" Jay Thomas said. "Would you tell me to just have faith alone, and say the sinner's prayer?"

"You know what, Jay, I was told that was true by several people at the Victory Baptist Church, but I'm not really so sure about it now. You know Cordell the barber?

"He's one of my relatives and he gave me a Bible and asked me to take it home and read some verses out of it. He had underlined several verses in the Bible he gave me and one of the passages he asked me to read was James 2:18. When I read that passage I noticed that this was one that Cordell had underlined. I thought it must have been pretty special for him to do that.

"Are you familiar with that passage, Jay? It's about the devil having faith."

"Yeah, I remember it," Jay Thomas said. "Wait a minute and let's get one of Mrs. Tipton's Bibles and read it."

Jay picked up a Bible laying on the end table just inside the front door. "Here's one," he said. "It's no wonder Cordell underlined this verse. Did you know that this is the only place in the Bible where you can find the words, *Faith only?*"

"Are you sure? I don't see how that can be. I've been told almost all my life that everybody is saved by faith only. That has to come out of the Bible."

"Well, right here in James 2 the Bible uses the words faith only, but it sure doesn't say faith only saves anybody. In fact, it is just the opposite. Look here at what it says."

James 2:19-20 (NKJV)

> *You believe that there is one God. You do well. Even the demons believe--and tremble! But do you want to know, O foolish man, that faith without works is dead?*

"And then here in verse 24 it says:"

You see then that a man is justified by works, and not by faith only.

"What do you think, Carl? Are the demons saved? They all have faith."

"No, there has to be something needed besides faith. What else could it be? Would it be the sinner's prayer?"

"Well, I hate to tell you this Carl, but the sinner's prayer is not in there either."

"Now wait a minute, Jay. I know you know a lot about the Bible, but that just can't be right. I was told by a Pastor of the church that all that was needed to be saved was faith alone and I needed to say the sinner's prayer. Surely he knows what the Bible says about being saved."

"OK, find it in the Bible then."

"How am I going to do that? I don't know everything in the Bible. I doubt that you do either. Jay Thomas, sometimes you aggravate me to no end."

"So you don't think that Baptist preacher could be wrong, do you? And you think if anybody's wrong it just has to be me. Well, then show me in the Bible where it says we are saved by the sinner's prayer or by faith alone."

"You know I can't do that. You know I can't put my finger on every word in the Bible, and neither can you."

"I can," Jay Thomas said.

I looked up at Jay Thomas and his expression had not changed. "Are you serious?" I said.

"Sure I can and you can too," he said.

"How can I do that?" I asked.

"Did you know that you can use a good Bible concordance and you can look up every word in the Bible and you can see every verse where it is used?"

"Wow, no, I didn't know that. Have you got a concordance like that?"

"Yeah, I sure do. I have one at home. Lots of people have them. There is a pretty good one right here in this Bible we are using. You probably have one in your own Bible.

"Look in the back of the Bible in the concordance and see if you can find any place where you can find the words *faith only or faith alone.*"

I turned to the back of the Bible and sure enough, there was the concordance just like he said. I tried the combination of words and it was there and it was listed, *faith only.*

"It is here," I said.

"How many times?" Jay Thomas said.

"Well, the word faith is here several times. But the words together as *faith only* are only here once."

"So it's found one time, is it? Well, what's the reference? Where is the verse where it's found?"

"Oh, well, never mind. The place where it's found is James 2:24. We just read that a few minutes ago. Is it possible for that to be the only place where faith only is found in the Bible? All that says is that faith only does not save us."

"Well Carl, I can tell you from my own search that you won't find it anywhere else. The Bible just does not tell us that we're saved by faith only. People don't get that idea from the Bible. It's just not there."

"You may be right, Jay. I'll keep looking for it, but I don't think it's there."

"Well, that brings us back to my original question then. What must I do to be saved? If you remember what you read in the Bible the other day, you need to be ready to give me an answer for the hope of salvation that's in you."

"What about the sinner's prayer, Jay. Is it in the Bible?"

"I'm sorry Carl, you won't find that either."

"Jay, if you're right about this, I may not even be saved myself. Cordell said I wasn't saved. And right now I can't even answer the question for myself."

Chapter 12   **Stealing Cherries**

Jay Thomas' questions were having an effect on my conscience and I was troubled over whether or not I really was saved. His tactic of making me read the Bible and study for myself was actually working to make me study the Bible. Not many nights went by that I didn't try to read at least a verse or two. Sometimes I would read several chapters if there was a story line I could follow. I wouldn't say that this reading didn't help me. I'm sure it did. But at this stage in my life, I did not have the overall picture of the Gospel sorted out to make good sense of what I read. Years later this would mean so much more to me.

But a day came when one of the boys who lived in the village asked me to spend the night with him and camp out in the woods behind his house. I knew Roger Johnson from school and from living not much over a mile from his house. I told Roger I would come if Rex could come with me. Roger had no problem with that and so the plans were made. For some reason, Linda didn't like the idea that Rex and I were getting ready to camp out with Roger Johnson. She just flat didn't like Roger and that seemed unfair to me. Later I would find out for myself what kind of boy Roger was.

The weekend came and Roger had a 4 man tent that he had used in the Boy Scouts and we set it up. We all took food and snacks and we had enough for a small group to probably last a week in the wilderness.

We built a nice big fire and sat around it and listened to a radio that Rex had brought with him. On Friday nights Everett High School had a radio program on a local AM station and students from the school acted as announcers and disk jockeys and played the latest rock and roll hits of the day.

You could dedicate a record to your girlfriend and they would announce the dedication on the radio and give the person's name that was making the dedication and the name of the person who it was dedicated to. If your name was mentioned on the radio and someone dedicated a song to you, you became the Monday morning celebrity when you went back to school. If a girl's name was mentioned, she was surrounded by a group of girls on Monday who could not wait to hear the whole story about who was dating who, and who was going steady with who. It was the same for the guys if a girl dedicated a song to you.

Everyone in the school listened to the Everett High broadcast. It would have been a disaster if you had missed your name on the radio.

We watched the lights to the houses go out one by one as the night wore on but we were way too excited to be sleepy. Sometime around midnight, Roger said, "How would you guys like some cherries?"

"You got cherries?" Rex said.

"No, but I know where to get some." Roger said.

"Where?"

"Ted Gilbert's tree." Roger said.

"Does he let you get cherries off his tree?" I said.

"He won't know anything about it. His lights went off a long time ago."

"Now wait a minute, Roger. Do you mean you want us to steal cherries off the Gilberts tree in their back yard? I don't think that's a good idea."

"He don't even pick those cherries. I raid that tree all the time. The birds get the most of them. I'll bet he ain't made 2 pies this year off that tree."

"What if he caught us? How would we explain that to everybody?"

"That old man won't even know we're there. You guys just stay outside the fence and watch the house and I'll go over to the tree and grab the cherries."

"I don't know. What do you think, Rex?"

"You can count me out. I don't want any part of it. You can go if you want too."

"I'll tell you what, Roger. I think Rex is right. I don't want to get involved in it either. I'm just going to wait right here with Rex. If you're going to steal cherries, count me and Rex out."

"I can't believe you guys are so chicken. What difference will a few cherries make that'll probably just be eat up by birds anyway? You both just wait right here and I'll be back in a few minutes."

The few minutes turned into almost an hour. In fact, Rex said that he probably got mad and went home. Rex was aggravated at Roger anyway over the cherries and he would have been just as happy if Roger didn't come back. But just as we made up our mind that he was not coming back, he appeared out of the dark.

"Did you steal the cherries?" Rex asked.

"Cherries? No, I didn't go over the fence at the Gilbert's house."

"You didn't get the cherries? Where in the world have you been?" I said. "You were gone over an hour. We figured you went home."

"Nah, I just walked around some of the houses over there and I came back. I didn't even bother with the cherries."

"Well good, I'm glad you didn't get any. I feel better about it. I don't like the idea of taking something that's not ours."

The rest of the night was pretty much uneventful and we finally went to sleep about one or two o'clock in the morning. We slept late Saturday morning and eventually we packed up the tent and our gear and headed home. All in all it was a lot of fun, but on the way home Rex made up his mind that this would be the last time he would pal around with Roger Johnson. I wasn't quite so dogmatic as Rex and I was more willing to give Roger a chance. Later on, I would regret that I ever knew him at all.

Monday morning came and I had hardly made it through my first class and headed down the hall to Mrs. Eunice Armstrong's algebra class, when I encountered Linda in the hall way.

"Do you know what people are saying about you and Rex today?"

"No I don't, what are they saying?"

"I've heard it from 2 or 3 people already. They say you and Rex helped Roger Johnson rob the preacher's house."

"What! Are you sure they're talking about us?"

"Yeah, they sure are. I've heard 2 people say that somebody seen you boys camping out in the woods and they said somebody else saw Roger Johnson going through the window of the Methodist preacher's house."

"They don't know what they're talking about. Roger was with me and Rex and we didn't have anything to do with robbing any house. Somebody's telling lies about us."

"If I were you, Carl, I'd go down to the principal's office and see what's going on. I saw the cops down there this morning when I first got here."

"I think I will. I want my name cleared before this goes any further."

I made my way past Mrs. Armstrong's class and went straight to the principal's office. Even before I walked through the office door, I could see through the large windows into the office and I could see Roger sitting in a chair. He seemed to be looking straight down at the floor and he was surrounded by two deputy sheriffs. I can't tell you how much this vision shook me. A bolt of fear went through my body and I suddenly felt weak all over. All at once I was struck by the seriousness of this situation I was walking into. I hesitated as I took hold of the office door handle and for a moment I had a panic that almost caused me to run. Mr. Davis, the principal saw me through the glass and I would guess that he could see the shear panic that was in my face. He walked to the door and opened the door for me and in a calm and gentle voice (which I thought was not like his normal tone) he said, "Carl come into my office for a minute."

We walked right past Roger and the deputies and we entered the private office of Mr. Davis, the principal.

"Carl, Roger confessed. He took the money at Reverend Newman's house Friday night while you boys were camping out. He told us that you and Rex didn't have anything to do with it."

"Did he say he did it? I don't see how he could have robbed anybody. He was with me and Rex all night."

"Well, according to Roger, he left you boys at the tent for awhile and went off by himself. Do you remember anything like that?"

"Yeah, now that you mention it, he did go off without me and Rex and he was gone a long time. He was gone so long that we thought he got mad and went home." (I didn't mention the part about the cherries).

"Well as far as I am concerned, you and Rex are in the clear. You can go on back to class. Ask Mrs. Hackberry for a hall pass to go back to class. But I would expect your buddy Roger is in more trouble than he knows what to do with."

"He's not really my buddy. That was the first time I had ever done anything with him. I should have listened to Linda Tipton. She told me not to be around him but I didn't think she was being fair, judging him like that."

"I'm afraid this may not be over for you, Carl. People have already started the rumor that you and Rex were involved with Roger. Rumors like that are hard to stop. People may whisper about this for a long time. Let this be a hard lesson for you to be careful and guard your friendships carefully. Many times you are judged by what your friends do."

I could see that he was right about that. That advice stayed with me the rest of my life.

When I went home I told daddy the whole story. He listened carefully but he had very little to say in the way of advice. That was his personality. He seldom told me what I needed to do and I was usually left to make my own decisions about how I handled things for myself. Looking back on this, I can see that this actually helped me to be able to take care of myself and to mature my own decision making ability. But he did have one piece of advice that actually helped me. Not so much with this immediate problem, but with my understanding of things about the church.

"If I were you, Carl, I'd go down there and talk to that preacher and tell him you didn't have anything to do with robbing his house."

And I did.

Chapter 13　The Methodist Preacher

Reverend Newman's house really wasn't all that far from mine. It was a small, plain house pretty much like all the other Eagleton Village houses. And Mr. and Mrs. Newman were really nice and friendly people. When I got there they invited me into their house and made me feel at ease and welcome. Mrs. Newman busied herself with bringing me a bottled coke and a plate of some of the most delicious cookies you ever tasted. I'm pretty sure she baked them herself because the whole house smelled like cake. Whatever she was cooking would make your mouth water just to sit there and smell that cake.

"We know you and Rex didn't have anything to do with taking the money the other night. The sheriff's deputies told us that Roger confessed, and he told them how he did it. We got our money back and so as far as we are concerned it was just misguided teenage boy making a mistake. I told the sheriff to go easy on him and maybe he's learned his lesson."

I could see that Reverend Newman was a kind gentle man. I had doubts about Roger, though. And as time went on, my gut feeling about him was right. After we all graduated from high school, Roger was arrested for trying to rob a bank up in Newport with a hawk bill knife. Roger spent most of his life in prison.

The Newman's were an older couple and their house looked decorated in an older style that I was not used to. The tables were covered with large white crocheted doilies that looked like Mrs. Newman had made them herself and the curtains were heavy and covered with tassels and lace and they were an old looking maroon color that reminded me of the curtains for the auditorium at the Everett High School stage. The house had an air of dignity, I thought, and the stateliness of it all was impressive to me. There were books in the bookshelves, more than I had ever seen in someone's house and almost every table seemed to have a Bible placed on it. It was pretty obvious to me that this man was a preacher and his house showed that he was a man of God.

"Carl, do you go to church anywhere?" he said.

"Well, I used to be a member of Victory Baptist Church," I said. "But it's been a long time since we moved from there. I doubt that they still consider me a member now."

"Well, Mrs. Newman and I would be happy for you to go to church with us. You know I'm the minister of the Methodist church over on the Old Knoxville Hwy., don't you?"

"Yeah, I knew you were a preacher. I didn't know where your church was but Mr. Davis, the principal, told me you were a Methodist."

"Do you think you would like to go to church with us? You'd be welcome to go."

"I don't know, Mr. Newman. To tell you the truth, I've been studying some of the things I was taught in the Baptist church and I'm not as convinced as I was that all of it was really true."

"What seems to be troubling you about it, Carl? Maybe I can help with some of it."

"Well for one thing I was told that people are saved by faith only. But it was pointed out to me that the words *faith only* are only found in the Bible one time and that's in James chapter 2 and that clearly says that we are not saved by faith only."

"Well Carl, if we are not saved by faith, then how are we saved?"

"That's a good question. I'm not sure. That's one of the things that bothers me.

"In James 2 it also says that the devil has faith, and we sure know that he's not saved. But that's not the only thing that bothers me about what I was told in the Baptist church."

"What else bothers you?"

"Well, I was told by Reverend Milsaps that even though most denominations teach different doctrines it really doesn't make any difference what they teach. He said God approves of all of their doctrines even if they are all different.

"Even then, I wondered how this could be.

"But since then, it was pointed out to me that the Bible says in Galatians chapter 1 that God says that if anyone preaches any other Gospel than the one Paul preached then let him be accursed.

"Can I use your Bible there on the table for a minute?"

I picked up the Bible and suddenly I wished I had Cordell's Bible handy. This verse was underlined in Cordell's Bible and it would be easier to find. But with a slight fumble and struggle, I did find the passage of scripture.

"Here it is," I said. "Listen to this."

Galatians 1:8-9 (KJV)

But though we, or an angel from heaven, preach any other gospel unto you than that which we have preached unto you, let him be accursed.

As we said before, so say I now again, If any man preach any other gospel unto you than that ye have received, let him be accursed.

"And that passage is just part of what bothers me about this. There's another one that bothers me even more. I forget just where it was found, but it was Jesus' prayer on the night he was betrayed."

"That would probably be in the book of John. It's somewhere around the 17th or 18th chapter."

That knowledge impressed me and made me have even more respect for Mr. Newman. It was plain to see that he knew his Bible.

I fumbled through chapter 17, reading as fast as I could and sure enough it was there in verse 20.

"Here it is," I said. "Listen to this."

John 17:20-21 (NKJV)

"I do not pray for these alone, but also for those who will believe in Me through their word;

that they all may be one, as You, Father, are in Me, and I in You; that they also may be one in Us, that the world may believe that You sent Me.

"It seems to me that if this is something that Jesus prayed about when He was about to die, then this is something we ought to listen to today."

"Well Carl, it sounds like there's a real struggle going on inside you with the Holy Spirit. I'll tell you what I think. I think you're struggling with the *illumination of the Spirit*."

"*The illumination of the Spirit?* What does that mean?"

"Well most scholars agree today with the interpretations of a great number of the founders of most of the mainstream denominations. They have determined that the Bible teaches us that the *natural man*, the man who does not have the Holy Spirit, cannot understand the things that God wants him to do. In fact, he's not even capable of understanding things about God until the Holy Spirit indwells him and enlightens his understanding of Spiritual things. That's called *The illumination of the Spirit*."

"I heard something similar to that at the Baptist church. I was told by one person that I would know when the Spirit came into my life. But I never seemed to feel anything that seemed to tell me that the Spirit was in me."

"Well Carl, you do have to use some logic and common sense at the same time. You may not feel the Spirit working in you but you will be able to see the results. At some point the Spirit will illuminate the gifts God has placed in you and you'll discover your true mission God has in store for you.

"We all have different gifts and talents for our service to God. God doesn't expect us to all be alike and do the same thing. We may not even see the Bible alike but we will see the parts that help us to fulfill the mission He has in store for us.

"The Holy Spirit will help you and illuminate your understanding of your gifts and your own personal place in your walk with God. There's no point in worrying about what someone else believes and what someone else thinks the Bible means. If you have the Spirit of God, you really only need to understand what God wants you to do in your own personal service and your own personal walk.

"Here's a Scripture that you might find interesting."

Mr. Newman took the Bible I was holding and quickly turned to 1 Corinthians chapter 2.

1 Corinthians 2:14 (KJV)
But the natural man receiveth not the things of the Spirit of God: for they are foolishness unto him: neither can he know them, because they are spiritually discerned.

"Wow, that's pretty complicated." I said.

"Yeah, it is complicated. The Bible is a complicated book. Not many people can really understand what they read. That's why men go to seminary school for several years before they become preachers."

"Say Carl, on another subject, do you ever do any yard work for any of your neighbors? I would like to get someone to mow my yard about once every week or so. If you have an interest in that I'll pay you to mow it for me. I have a mower. It's pretty old but it works."

"Sure, I'll be glad to mow it for you. How about Saturday?"

"Fine, I'll see you Saturday."

On the way home I thought about what Mr. Newman had said. It all seemed so complicated and scholarly that at first I didn't even consider questioning any of it. But as I thought about it as I walked, a couple of things seemed a little out of place to me. For instance, if the Holy Spirit illuminates a person and tells him the true meaning of the Bible and religious things, then how could it be that people would all see the same things different? Somehow that just didn't seem logical at all to me. If that was the case then what would we do with that passage in Galatians that says *if anyone preaches a different Gospel let him be accursed?* How could we just ignore this Scripture as though it had no meaning?

And not only that, would it really make any sense for people to claim that they had been illuminated with understanding from the Holy Spirit and then have churches with different doctrines? I don't see how this could be a logical explanation at all.

And another thing. Why would a person have to go to seminary school in order to understand the Bible if the Holy Spirit had illuminated him with understanding?

What's wrong with me, I thought. Could it be that the Holy Spirit is struggling inside me like Mr. Newman said? Could it be that the devil is preventing me from understanding these things? I shuddered when I thought about the devil preventing me from understanding how to be saved. These things troubled me as I took the long walk home.

By Saturday I was ready to mow the Newman's yard. He really didn't tell me how much money he would pay me for the job, but I usually charged two dollars and I expected it would be somewhere near that amount.

As I walked up the driveway I could see that the yard was really overdue to be mowed. Mr. Newman must have fertilized the grass heavy because it was exceptionally green and tall. I knew just by looking that this would be a hard yard to mow. Not only was the grass thick and wet, the back yard had quite a slope to it. It would be hard to push a mower up that hill.

Mr. Newman already had the mower and the gas can sitting in the driveway waiting on me to get there and I could see that he had mowed a little part of the front yard. The grass had clumped up and made a big mess where he had mowed. This yard will take a lot of raking, I thought. It's a good thing it's not very big.

I knocked on the front door and Mr. Newman came out holding a huge 3 pound stubby hammer in his hand.

"Good morning, Carl. I was just about to make a little adjustment on the lawnmower for you. I tried to mow a little and the grass is so tall and thick that the mower won't blow the grass out the chute. I'm going to knock the back out of the mower deck and the grass can just clump up all it wants to and it won't have to blow out the chute. We'll just rake it up when we get it mowed."

"Sounds good to me," I said.

And with a couple of swift blows from the big hammer the entire back of the lawnmower deck was busted out. This worked very well, actually, and I mowed most of the yard during the next two hours.

Things went well. That is, until.

Until I started to mow up and down the hill in the back yard. Going up the hill was hard. But going down the hill seemed easy. Easy, that is, until my foot slipped in the wet grass. My foot slipped and of all places for it to slide, it went right through the big busted out place in the back of the lawnmower deck that Mr. Newman had just busted out.

You would have thought that there would have been pain, but there wasn't. I felt the blade hit my foot and it was so hard that the mower actually stalled out and stopped. My tennis shoe was ripped to shreds in an instant and there was blood all over my foot. I couldn't walk and I fell and rolled on the ground. I'm not sure what kind of noise I made but both Mr. and Mrs. Newman came running out of the house at the same time. The look on their faces told me the story. My foot was hurt bad, that was easy to tell.

Mrs. Newman ran back into the house and in a flash she was back with scissors and a towel and a big box of salt. She seemed to know what she was doing and it was plain to see that Mr. Newman let her take over and be in charge of the emergency. She cut the rest of the tennis shoe and sock off my foot and she held pressure on the wound just long enough to soak up the blood with the towel and she poured about half of the big box of salt directly on the wounds in my foot. There still was no pain. I guess that the blow to my foot had deadened all the nerves long enough for Mrs. Newman to administer her first aid.

I still couldn't walk without help and Mr. and Mrs. Newman half carried me to their car and we made a bee line to the Blount County Emergence Room.

As bad as this could have been, the emergence room doctor said that my foot would be alright.

It was plenty sore for several weeks, but it did get well and it never gave me any trouble after that.

I was paid five dollars for that mowing job, which was more than I would have charged if things had gone right.

Over the next year or two I mowed this yard several times and I was paid five dollars every time. I liked the Newman's. I never did go to church with them but they were a really nice couple. I think she was one of the best cooks I ever knew. Her house always smelled like cake.

Chapter 14   The Woodpecker Gospel

My foot was sore for almost a month after the lawnmower incident but I was able to walk on it in just a couple of days. I limped a little for awhile but there was no lasting effect.

I went to church on a Wednesday night with Rex and Linda and the Tipton family not too long after my discussion with Mr. Newman. Jay Thomas was there and Mr. Hall was still the teacher of the class. By now I knew all the kids in the class, most of them from school. There was Patsy Day who lived about 2 blocks from me in the village and there was Ann Cartwright and Joyce Turner and many others. All of these young people were destined to be my best friends for the next few years all through high school and even after I moved from Tennessee when I graduated.

Tonight Mr. Hall started the class with the question, ***"Does God have authority over the wind?"***

I think most people know the answer to that question and I don't think Mr. Hall really wanted an answer; he just wanted us to think about it. We all said, "Yes, He does!"

"Ok, then if that is the case with the wind, ***does God Have authority over the universe?"***

By now people in the class were comfortable with the way the questions were going and the answer was, once again, "Yes, He does!"

"So with all of this in mind, and with the understanding that it is the natural order of things for the universe and everything in it to be subject to the authority of God, what would you expect to do if God commanded you to do something? Would you do it?"

It was almost like a light bulb of logic went off in my head. Robert Hall was one of the most logical teachers I ever had.

"So," Mr. Hall continued, "If God wanted to give you any instructions or tell you something He wanted you to do, how do you think He would get the message to you?"

I thought about what Mr. Newman had said to me about the *illumination of the Spirit* and about the *natural man* not being able to understand Spiritual things until the Spirit came into him and illuminated his understanding. I had already felt some apprehension about the logic of that explanation and I couldn't wait for the rest of the explanation about this understanding of God's message to us.

"Where do we get God's message and instruction for us? It's written for us to read in the Bible. Look at what the Bible has to say about what the Scriptures can do for us. Open you bible to 2 Timothy 3:16."

I turned to the passage as quickly as I could, anticipating and wondering, would this be one of those passages that Cordell had underlined? It was.

2 Timothy 3:16-17 (NKJV)

All Scripture is given by inspiration of God, and is profitable for doctrine, for reproof, for correction, for instruction in righteousness, that the man of God may be complete, thoroughly equipped for every good work.

"So, what does this Scripture tell us that the Bible can do for us?" Mr. Hall continued. "Notice that it tells us we can use the Bible for doctrine, reproof, for correction and for instruction in righteousness? And as if that wasn't enough, there's more. Jay Thomas, tell them what else is in this verse."

Jay Thomas hadn't said much up to this point, but when he did start his explanation of the rest of the verse, I was suddenly confident that his knowledge of the Bible was almost as good, or maybe just as good, as was Mr. Hall's.

I developed a respect for Jay Thomas' knowledge of the Bible in this class and I was never disappointed in things he said.

"Well, all those things that we just mentioned are important. They're things that the Bible does for us. But that's not all. Look at what the last part of the verse says, and this is highly important and significant to us all. It says that we don't need anything else other than the Bible to make us complete. Look at what it says:"

that the man of God may be complete, thoroughly equipped for every good work.

"So what this tells us is that we don't need any other books or writings to equip us for any good work. The Bible is all we need. We don't need any special revelations or divine messengers like angels. And we don't need some special gift from God over and above the Bible to guide us in what we need to know and what we need to do."

"That's right, Jay," Mr. Hall said. "The Bible is complete and it is all we need. But if we read something in the Bible that God wants us to do, how important is it for us to obey God's instructions and do it?"

"If we want to know the answer to that question, based on what we just read, then we would find the answer in the Bible," I said.

"Good answer, Carl. That makes sense, doesn't it? If God wants us to know, then it should be found in the Bible. So where in the Bible would we find how important is it for us to obey God's instructions?"

"Try Hebrews 5:9," Jay Thomas said. "It's not just important. Our very salvation depends on it."

Hebrews 5:9 (NKJV)

9 And having been perfected, He became the author of eternal salvation to all who obey Him,

"This verse is talking about Jesus," Mr. Hall said. "Jay Thomas is right. It says plainly here that salvation is for those who obey Christ. Now this is the positive side and it says **we'll be saved if we obey Christ."**

"But there is a negative side, too. We can be lost if we don't obey Christ. Look at Ephesians 5:6."

Ephesians 5:6 (NKJV)

6 Let no one deceive you with empty words, for because of these things the wrath of God comes upon the sons of disobedience.

"Look at what happens to those people who disobey God's instructions. Would anyone want the wrath of God?"

"Mr. Hall," Joyce said. "I've heard people say that if our heart is sincere and we love God, then doing everything just like the Bible tells us to do it is not so important. That is, as long as we are sincere in our love for God."

"Joyce, whoever told you that, doesn't have a clear understanding of what the love of God really is. You really can't separate the words love and obedience when you are talking about God. Open your Bibles to 1 John 5:2."

1 John 5:2-3 (NKJV)

2 By this we know that we love the children of God, when we love God and keep His commandments.

3 For this is the love of God, that we keep His commandments. And His commandments are not burdensome.

"Let's review what we've learned in class tonight. We only have a couple of minutes left. First off, we learned that just like all of God's creation, we're all required to be subject to God's authority. That means we're required to obey God's instructions in the all the things He tells us to do.

"And we also learned that anything God wants us to know, He reveals to us in the Bible. The Bible is complete and it is all we need to instruct us in how we live our lives and how to do what God wants us to do.

"We also learned that we have to obey God in order to be saved. And we read that those who don't obey God are subject to not being saved.

"And last, but not least, we discovered that obedience to the authority of God is the same thing as our love for God.

"Any questions?"

He no more than said that, when the bell rang ending the class. But the class was silent and for just a moment no one moved. It was almost as if no one wanted the class to end and so we waited in our seats.

"You can go," Mr. Hall said.

And suddenly, the class was over.

Jay Thomas had the car again tonight and we headed for Richy Kreme to hang out. On the way out of the parking lot we saw Linda Tipton and Joyce Turner at the Tipton's car. They were headed to Richy Kreme with Mrs. Tipton and the girls. We asked them to go with us and it was an easy decision which Mrs. Tipton agreed to, providing we had the girls home by eleven.

Richy Kreme had curb service and there was always rock and roll music playing out of the speakers under the shelter roof. Linda sat in the front seat with Jay and Joyce sat with me in the back. Joyce was a nice Christian girl but she was beautiful and there was no doubt in her mind about that.

She had self confidence to spare. And she had a way of looking into my eyes and taking my hand in hers and talking in a soft voice. And then with a flash she would be distracted by some friend at school and out of the car she would flit. Off to another car parked close by and into the car she would go with some girl on a date with her boyfriend. She was the perfect picture of a beautiful teenage girl standing beside the car at a curb service ice cream joint. She was the center of attention, and she knew it.

We sat for a long time and we took Joyce home in time to get Linda home by eleven. Jay and I didn't have the same curfew as the girls and so we headed off to the Dixie Drive in. Dixie was almost the same type of place as Richy Kreme but they stayed open until 12:30. Most of the cars were gone when we parked at the curb service microphone. We ordered cokes and just sat to talk.

"Jay, I was impressed with the Bible class tonight. I learned more than I did the whole time I was at Victory Baptist Church. And not only that, I think some of the things they taught me may not be right."

"Why do you say that? Have you learned something different?"

"Yeah, I think I have. Actually, quite a few things."

"Like what?"

"Well for one thing, I was told that I was saved by faith only when I said the sinner's prayer. Ever since you and I talked about that, I have looked for someone to show me where that's found in the Bible, and the only place where it's found says that we are not saved by faith only. And now based on what we read tonight about the Bible being complete and it's all we need for instruction in our obedience to God, if the sinner's prayer and salvation by faith only are not in the Bible then they are not valid

Bible teaching. I think somebody just made those doctrines up. I don't think they are found in the Bible at all.

"And that's not all. I've been told by two preachers that the Bible is not simple enough for a regular person to read and discover what God wants us to do. I have been told that the Holy Spirit has to come into your heart and illuminate your understanding so you can understand Spiritual things. And yet tonight we all read that the Bible is complete and it is all we need for instruction. But even before I read that tonight I had my doubts that Spiritual illumination was a true doctrine. If it was, then why would there be so many churches with different doctrines? Why would the Holy Spirit tell one church one doctrine and then tell another church some different doctrine?

"I was told by the Pastor at Victory Baptist that even though churches saw things different and didn't see the Bible alike, every one of the mainstream denominations are approved and acceptable to God. And here we are tonight reading out of the Bible that our salvation depends on our being obedient to God's instructions.

"I've been given every type of explanation you could imagine to all the questions I've asked people about religion. The only thing that even makes sense in any logical way at all is when I read the answer out of the Bible."

Jay Thomas sat quietly until I finished, and then he looked at me and he sort of smiled. I'll never forget what he said.

"Well Carl, I can tell you what your trouble is. **You're listening to the woodpecker Gospel.**"

"What do you mean; I'm listening to the woodpecker Gospel? What are you talking about?"

"Well, there's a story that has been made famous by one of our old time Gospel preachers, Foy Smith, about woodpeckers.

"It seems that an old fellow had a hog lot up in the woods behind his house and one day a neighbor was walking down the road and he noticed that all the hogs were acting funny. The neighbor knocked on the door and told the old fellow that his hogs were running from tree to tree and stopping and listening and running all over the lot like they were confused.

"The old fellow said, 'oh well, I know what's wrong with 'em. I used to take their feed out to the lot and I'd holler for the hogs and they'd all run to my voice and I'd feed 'em. But here lately I've lost my voice and I can't holler. So I've been taking my walking stick up to the lot and pecking on the side of a tree and they would come to that sound. But last week a bunch of woodpeckers moved in up there and now they just don't know what to do!'

"That's your problem, Carl. Every time you ask a question the woodpeckers start pecking on the trees and you don't know who to listen to."

"You know, that's funny. But you just may be right. That pretty much describes what's going on alright."

"Well you know what you have to do, don't you?"

"No, what?"

"What you should have been doing all along. Get your answers out of the Bible. You just said that it's the only thing that's made any sense."

"I think you're right Jay. In fact, I know you are. The Bible is the only place, so far, where any answers I've got seem to make any logical sense. Somehow, that just don't seem to be right, does it? I mean, you would think asking a pastor of a church would be the same thing as reading the answer out of the Bible, but I can see it's not. **Starting now, if I ask a question, I want to read the answer from the Bible, myself.**"

Chapter 15 Cordell's Teaching

Rex came by on Saturday morning and wanted me to go with him to get a haircut. Daddy overheard what Rex said about a haircut and offered to drive us both over to Cordell's barber shop since he had to go to Maryville anyway. That suited me just fine. I hadn't been in Cordell's shop since he gave me the Bible and I really wanted to tell him how much I had enjoyed using it. There was a small barber shop on the Old Knoxville Hwy. run by Bob Woods' father and I had been going there because of Bob. It was close and handy and I liked Bob as a friend. Bob and I rabbit hunted together as often as we could.

On one hunting trip Bob's beagles were hot on a rabbit's trail and I climbed to the top of a sawdust pile at an old abandoned sawmill to try to get a shot at the rabbit. If you've ever watched beagles trail a rabbit, you know that in every case the rabbit always runs a big circle and comes right back to where the dogs jumped him up at the start. That's what I was expecting when I climbed the sawdust pile to get a place high enough to watch for the rabbit. What I didn't expect to see was smoke drifting up between my legs out of the sawdust. Suddenly it dawned on me that the sawdust pile was on fire. That's not really unusual. Sawdust piles are notorious for catching fire due to spontaneous combustion and smoldering for months. Many times the whole interior of the sawdust pile will be smoldering in a big cauldron of fire. I knew all that when I looked down and saw the smoke coming up around my feet. I knew that if the crust gave way I could fall into a cauldron of hot coals. I was lucky. I got off the sawdust without breaking through. But when Bob got there with the dogs, he grabbed a pole and jammed it into the sawdust and the whole area flamed up in fire.

Bob and I hunted together many times and he was a good friend. I went to his dad's barber shop most of the time to get a haircut.

But daddy used Cordell as his barber and that's where he took me and Rex today. The shop wasn't too busy when we got there. That was unusual because there were usually several guys waiting on a Saturday to get haircuts. In fact, there was only one guy in front of us and he went fast. I was next.

"Howdy, Carl," he said in his usual friendly tone. "I was just talking to Pete last week about you." (Pete was a nickname our family used for my daddy. His name was Clarice but for some reason, which no one seemed to remember, the family called him Pete) "I told him to bring you in here for a haircut."

"Thanks, Cordell. I've been laying off to come in here myself. I wanted to tell you about the Bible you gave me."

"Oh yeah, the Bible. What do you think of it?"

"Are you kidding? It's great! It's one of the best things anybody ever gave me. I've used that Bible more than you could ever imagine."

"Man, that's great. I had a feeling you'd get some good use out of it. That's why I wanted you to have it."

"You know what I really like about it?"

"What?"

"I like the fact that so many of the verses are underlined. It seems like every time I encounter one of those underlined verses, I learn something that's important. Did you underline the verses?"

"Yeah, I did. You ought to do that too, Carl. Every time you encounter a verse that has a special meaning to you, you should underline it. That makes it easier to go back to it and remember it."

"Well, so far, the ones I've found that have been important to me have already been underlined by you. I like that."

"Ha, don't worry. As you study the Bible, you'll find your own verses to underline."

"Say, are you still going to that Baptist church?"

"Well, no. It's been a long time since I went there. I doubt that they still consider me a member by now."

"Really? Are you going to church anywhere?"

"Yeah, I've been going with Rex some. His mama takes me with them."

"So you've been going to church with the Tiptons? Man, that's great, Carl. You keep that up. That's a good place for you to learn something about the Bible. I know Robert Wilson, he's a good preacher."

"Well, I have learned some things since I've been there. You know, Cordell, when I was here and you gave me the Bible, I had just been baptized and I told you I was saved by faith. Do you remember that you told me that I might not be saved at all?"

"What have you learned since you've been going with the Tiptons?"

"Well for one thing, I was told by Reverend Milsaps at the Victory Baptist Church that I was saved by faith. And I've learned that the Bible tells us in James chapter 2 that the devil has faith and we know he's not saved. So I've questioned and doubted that the Bible supports the idea that we are saved by faith alone."

"Well, that's partly right, Carl. There's nowhere in the Bible where we're told that we're saved by faith alone. The fact is *we are not saved by faith alone*. But that's not all there is to it. We are not saved by any *one thing alone*."

"Are you saying that we are saved by more than one thing?"

"Yep, I sure am. But let's talk about faith for a minute. We are saved by faith. The Bible tells us that we're saved by faith. That's been true ever since man was created and placed on the earth. Even Abraham was saved by faith. We are too. The Bible supports the teaching that we are saved by faith. The problem is this; men have misunderstood and twisted the Bible to try to make it say that we are saved by **faith alone.** That's where the error and false teaching comes in. The Bible tells us that we are saved by faith but it does not say that we are saved by faith alone."

"Cordell, is there a place in the Bible that tells us that we are saved by faith?"

"Sure! There're plenty of places that tell us that we have to have faith to be saved. What you won't find is any place where it tells us that we're saved by faith alone.

"Rex, pick up that Bible on the shelf and turn to Hebrews 11:6. Read what that says. You should notice that it's underlined."

Hebrews 11:6 (NKJV)
6 but without faith it is impossible to please Him, for he who comes to God must believe that He is, and that He is a rewarder of those who diligently seek Him.

"Notice that the verse says that **it's impossible to please God without faith?** It's always been like that. God has always required those who come to Him to have faith. If we read on further, the next verses from verse 7 through verse 12, we would see that the Bible says Noah had faith when he built the ark. It says Abraham, Isaac and Jacob all had faith as they obeyed God's instructions about the land of promise.

"And even Sarah had faith as she listened to God. God has always required faith in those people who He saves."

"Wow! That's interesting. Are there any more verses?"

"Sure, there's plenty. Almost everybody knows John 3:16. I'll bet you can quote it."

"I can," Rex said.

John 3:16 (NKJV)
16 for God so loved the world that He gave His only begotten Son, that whoever believes in Him should not perish but have everlasting life.

"I remember that," I said.

"Almost everybody can quote that verse," Cordell said. "The trouble is, almost all denominational churches use this verse to try to prove that we are saved by faith alone and that makes it a false doctrine and untrue."

"Well it does say that anyone who believes on Him will have everlasting life."

"Yes it says that. But this is not the only verse in the Bible that talks about everlasting life and salvation. Let's apply just a little logic and common sense to what this means. **Would this include the devil? We know the devil believes on Him, so is the devil saved?**"

"Now, let's read another verse. **This verse tells us why the devil is not saved.** The devil lacks something else that's also required to be saved. Rex, read Acts 3:19."

Acts 3:19 (NKJV)
19 Repent therefore and be converted, that your sins may be blotted out, so that times of refreshing may come from the presence of the Lord,

"What do you think this is talking about, Carl?"

"Well, it's pretty simple. It says repent and be converted in order to have your sins blotted out."

"Do you think you can be saved without having your sins blotted out?"

"No, I don't think you can. You can't be saved unless your sins are forgiven."

"Well, there you go. Now we know that the Bible tells us that we must have faith in order to be saved, but here we read where we have to repent and be converted in order to be saved. Now in case you don't know it, repentance means to make a decision to change your life and your thinking and make a commitment to live your life in obedience to God's instructions."

"There's another verse that's even stronger. Rex, read Luke 13:5."

Luke 13:5 (NKJV)
5 I tell you, no; but unless you repent you will all likewise perish."

"What do you think, Rex? Is repentance required in order to be saved?"

"It looks as clear as a bell to me, Cordell. You couldn't have proved it any better. The Bible is really clear. Faith and repentance are both required in order to be saved. ***But I happen to know something else that's required, too.***"

I had learned more in the last 10 minutes than all that time I spent at Victory Baptist Church. And what's more, I had read it out of the Bible myself. And now, here I am, literally hungry for more Bible information about the subject of salvation and Rex tells me that there is still more to know.

"You're right, Rex. There's still more to know. God has given us a plan that He's designed for being saved. ***The Bible calls this plan of salvation, the Gospel.***"

"Rex, will you look up Romans 1:16?"

Romans 1:16 (NKJV)
16 for I am not ashamed of the gospel of Christ, for it is the power
of God to salvation for everyone who believes,

"Now Carl, a lot of people don't even know that this next step is even in the Bible. But the Bible tells us that we must be willing to publicly confess that Jesus is God's Son in order to be saved. There are accounts of people in the Bible who had a desire to become Christians, but they failed because they were afraid to confess Christ publicly for one reason or another."

By this time Cordell had finished cutting my hair and Rex handed the Bible to me and climbed up in the chair.

"Carl, you have the Bible now. Read Romans 10:10."

Romans 10:9-10 (NKJV)
9 that if you confess with your mouth the Lord Jesus and believe in
your heart that God has raised Him from the dead, you will
be saved.
10 For with the heart one believes unto righteousness, and with
the mouth confession is made unto salvation.

"Do you see the connection to salvation?"

"Yeah, it's pretty plain. It says that **confession is made unto salvation.** In other words, confession is part of the Gospel plan of salvation."

"Yep, that's right. There's other verses but that one tells it pretty plain. You can't be saved without confession. We know that because of what happened in John 12:42."

John 12:42-43 (NKJV)
42 Nevertheless even among the rulers many believed in Him, but
because of the Pharisees they did not confess Him, lest
they should be put out of the synagogue;
43 for they loved the praise of men more than the praise of God.

"So what have we learned so far, Carl? Here we've read the Bible for 15 minutes and look what a little logic and common sense have taught us."

"Well, let's see. We learned that a person must have faith in order to be saved. But we also learned that faith alone is not enough. It takes repentance and confession as well.

"You know, Cordell, maybe I was saved in the Baptist church after all. I have always had faith and I've been repentant for a long time. I have a genuine desire to follow God's instructions. I really do want to do things the way God wants me to. And I'm ready and willing to confess that Christ is God's son any time I need to. Does this make me saved?"

"I'm afraid it doesn't, Carl. There's still one more step in the Gospel plan of salvation. Now you may think you've already done it, but you haven't done it right. I remember that from the day I gave you the bible."

"Are you talking about baptism? I remember you mentioning baptism the day I was in here."

"Yep, that's exactly what I'm talking about. You need to know the real Bible meaning of baptism. Do you think you understand the purpose of baptism according to the Bible definition?"

"No, I'm not sure that I do. I was taught wrong about so many things that I made up my mind that anything else somebody wants to teach me has to be right there in the Bible for me to read. I need to read what the Bible has to say about baptism."

"Well, there's a lot in the Bible about baptism and what it's for. Why don't you start reading this when you get home today and then tomorrow when you go to church, I want you to ask Robert Wilson to tell you about baptism. I'm going to call him after awhile and ask him to talk to you."

By this time the haircuts were over. I saw daddy's car parked outside the barber shop and me and Rex made our way to the car. These few minutes of Bible study were some of the best I can ever remember. Cordell knew his Bible, I would sure give him credit for that. Looking back on this, I can see that he was a great influence on my life.

Daddy took one look at my hair and said, "Did you actually get a haircut? Your hair looks about as long as it did when I dropped you off."

There was no way he would ever like James Dean's hair style. I had hoped he wouldn't notice that I had very little taken off. Cordell was a barber and he knew the popular styles boys were wearing and so he didn't take much off and he left the sideburns long. I liked it that way. Most of the boys in school had theirs about like mine. I guess I was just like all teenage boys. I wanted to blend in to the popular culture of the day.

The first thing I saw as we turned the corner on Norris Street heading toward our house was Jay Thomas' car in front of our house. Rex said, "Hey, there's Jay's car in front of your house."

As we passed the car I could see that he wasn't inside and I could see Jay and Linda sitting on the metal glider in the Tipton's back yard. She had her head on Jay's shoulder.

"You know, Rex, if I didn't know better, I'd think Linda would like to be Jay Thomas' girlfriend."

"Don't ever tell her I said this," Rex said. "But she already thinks she is."

Chapter 16   **The Kidnapping**

Jay Thomas saw daddy's car pull up in our driveway and he saw me get out of the car. Rex went into his house and I walked out back where Linda and Jay were sitting on the glider.

"Hey Carl, we've been waiting on you," Linda said.

"Why, what's up?" I said.

"Would you like to ride up to the Top of the World?"

"Is that road finished? The last time I was up there with Bob Woods that road was nowhere near finished. It was nothing but dirt in places."

"Well, some of it is gravel and some of it is dirt but it's dry. We haven't had any rain for 2 weeks. And besides that, Joyce wants you to go."

"Joyce wants me to go? Where is she?"

Linda looked at me like I was a dunce and raised her head and looked up at the sky. "Are you so dumb that you don't understand this?"

"Understand what?"

"Carl, what she's trying to say is that Joyce wants you to call her and ask her to go."

"Are you sure about that? Does she even know that you're going?"

"What do you think? She's Linda's best friend."

"Do you think I should call her?"

"If you don't, I know 2 girls that are going to be plenty mad at you."

I called Joyce from Linda's kitchen phone. She did want to go. And not only that, I got the impression that she was waiting on a phone call from me.

Joyce's mother dropped her off at Linda's house. I doubted that her mother knew the entire plan. I'm not sure Linda's mother did either. Somehow, I suspected that if they had known where we were going they would have stopped the whole plan. But we didn't volunteer and they didn't ask.

Joyce was wearing black pedal pushers and a bright sky blue blouse that seemed to come together in the front with long sash like extensions that tied together with the ends hanging down in the front. And her long brown hair was pulled together into a pony tail with a matching blue ribbon tied around it to hold it in place. She was beautiful.

She had a mysterious power over me, of that there was no doubt. She radiated confidence every where she went. No boy could ignore her if she decided she wanted his attention, and she almost always did. She was flirtatious and fun, and she was a Christian. To her, everything was just innocent fun and harmless. She was full of life and she enjoyed the power her beauty had over boys.

It was 5:00 before we got started and it was a long way to the Foothills Parkway. And then to get to the new Top of The World road that was being built would be another good ½ hour. The road was 15 miles long and it went right along the top of the Chilhowee Mountain. That's why they called it the Top of The World.

By the time we got started up the Top of The World road it was already dark. The road was still under construction and there were trucks and dozers and heavy equipment setting everywhere. The banks along the road were steep and were bare dirt and we seemed to be the only people anywhere to be seen.

About 5 miles up the road we saw a light in the distance in the middle of the road.

Linda was the first to see it and she exclaimed, "Look, what is that light? It looks like a fire in the middle of the road."

"It is a fire," Jay Thomas said. "Somebody's got a bonfire in the middle of the road."

As we got closer we could see people standing around the fire, and it was obvious they were looking at us.

Jay Thomas pulled the car up closer to the fire and stopped. He left the motor running and we could see in the firelight what appeared to be 3 rough looking characters looking back at us. There were 3 large motorcycles parked on the side of the road near the fire and it was obvious that these were the bikes that belonged to the 3 men standing around the fire. For Jay Thomas and me, this was a dangerous situation to find ourselves in, especially with 2 girls in the car with us. Nobody had to tell us about the danger here; we knew what we were facing instantly and it was not a good place to be.

"Let's get out of here," I said.

"Wait," Joyce shouted. "Look at the motorcycles." And as she was shouting, she opened the rear door of the car and stepped out on the ground and headed toward the fire.

All three men saw her and they all came toward her at once. "Hey guys, are those your motorcycles? Wow, they look great."

One of the men, who looked to be in his mid twenties, spoke up. "Hey good looking, you like motorcycles? Take a look at that Indian job. That one's mine." He put his hand on Joyce's arm and led her to where the motorcycles were parked just outside the firelight.

This was Joyce's element. She had the attention of every one of these men. They were all around her and the motorbikes. She used all of her flirtation skills almost by instinct.

And they worked just as they were supposed to. These men sure had an interest in her.

It wasn't that she wanted anything bad to happen; it's just that she loved the power she had over boys and the attention that came with it.

"Say, honey, how would you like to take a ride on one?" the one guy said.

"I can't go for a ride with you. I don't even know you," Joyce said. But as she said it you could see the flirtatious mischief in her face and it was easy to see that she only wanted to be asked again. "Where would we go?" she said.

"Right up there to the top of the road and back. You won't be gone but a minute and you can see how you like it."

"Joyce, you need to stay here with us," Linda said.

"Why, he's just going up to the top of the hill and back. This won't take but a minute. We'll be right back."

Joyce got on the back of the motorcycle with the man and they took off. One of the other men got on his motorcycle at the same time and he followed them as they headed up the road.

We watched as the motorcycles got to the top of the hill where they were supposed to turn around and come back but they didn't even slow down. They went right over the hill and the head lights disappeared over the other side.

The third man was an older man and he stayed with the fire. Not a word was said until the older man spoke up. "If I were you I wouldn't let that young girl go off with them two guys. They're not the type you could trust with a girl like that."

"Get in the car," Jay Thomas said. In a flash we were all in the car and heading down the road following the motorcycles. By the time we topped the hill the two motorcycles were nowhere to be seen.

Jay Thomas gunned the car and tried to get more speed, but it was hard to do in the shape the new road was in. We drove for a good five miles and there was no sign of the motorcycles any where we could see. I looked behind us and I could see the headlight of one motorcycle coming up behind us.

"That must be the other guy coming up the road," I said.

Jay stopped the car and waited on the motorcycle to catch up. "We can't find them," I shouted out the window as he pulled up alongside.

"My guess is that they headed for Claybow's," he said.

"Where's Claybow's?" I asked

"Claybow's is a joint down on Six Mile Road," he said. "Take the paved secondary road to the right about 2 miles up the mountain. Follow it to Claybow's Place. Just follow me. I'll take you down there."

True to his word, he took us to Claybow's Beer Joint. Linda stayed in the car and locked the doors while Jay Thomas and I went into the joint. This was not a place we wanted to be. The music was loud and the beer flowed free. We saw Joyce sitting at a table in the back with the 2 bikers and we walked over where they were. The older guy went with us.

"Joyce, we're here to get you," I said.

Joyce stood up. There was a strange, frightened look on her face as she looked at us and she started to walk toward us. One of the guys put his hand on her arm and said, "Just a minute, honey, you're with us."

"No, I have to leave", she said.

"Come on, we have to leave now," Jay Thomas said. "We have to get you home."

"Are you boys looking for trouble?" the man said who had his hand on Joyce's arm.

At this point I don't know what would have happened to me and Jay Thomas if the older man hadn't stepped in for our defense. "Leave 'em alone, Denny," he said. "Let that girl go home. She's under age and ever one of us will be in big trouble if you mess with her."

"She wants to stay with me, don't you honey?"

"Leave me alone," Joyce said as she pulled her arm away from the guy called Denny. "I don't want anything to do with you. Stay away from me."

Denny stood up and by the look on his face I could see that this was about to escalate into a fight. I wasn't the only one to see the look on his face, the guy on the other side of the bar must have seen it too. "Hold on there Hoss, we won't have no fighting in here, you know that."

And then he looked straight at Jay Thomas and me and said, "How old are you boys? Are you boys 21?"

"We're trying to leave," Jay Thomas said. "We're here to get Joyce. We're taking her with us."

"She don't want to go," Denny said.

"Yes I do," Joyce said. "You brought me here without even asking me. I don't want to be here."

"Are you 21," the big guy said?

"No, I'm 17," Joyce said.

"Alright you boys take this girl and get out of here. Don't come back until you're 21."

At this, the guy named Denny sat back down at the table and Joyce ran to us and we all made a hasty exit out the door. Jay Thomas gunned his mama's car and we flew off down the highway not having a clue as to where this road would take us. Joyce began to cry. "I was so afraid," she said. "I didn't think anyone would even know where I was."

"We almost didn't," Linda said. "If it hadn't been for the older guy that was with them, we would never have found you. I hope you realize what a close call you had."

"I didn't think they would do anything like that," Joyce sobbed. "I was so afraid. It would have been awful if you hadn't come for me."

"You live a sheltered life, Joyce," Jay Thomas said. "You're surrounded by Christian friends and you have a Christian family. The whole world is not like that."

"I was so stupid. I see that now. Are you all mad at me? I owe you so much for finding me. There's no telling what would have happened to me if you hadn't found me."

"Well, I'm mad at you," Linda said. "I'm glad you're OK, but I'm mad at you. That was a stupid thing to do and not only did you get in trouble yourself but you put all of us in danger too. Do you realize Carl and Jay risked their own lives to go in there and bring you out?"

"I do and I'm sorry. You're right; it was a stupid thing to do." Linda gave Joyce a tissue to wipe her eyes and then she reached back over the seat and gave her a big hug.

By the time we got Linda and Joyce back to the Tipton's house it was almost 11:00. I couldn't believe that we actually made it before the curfew. We made an agreement between the four of us not to reveal the details of this encounter to anyone. I don't know if Linda or Joyce ever told their mothers, but they never asked me anything about it.

Jay and I decided not to go home just yet. He hadn't said much about what we had just experienced, but I could see that he was just as nervous and hyper about it as I was. We went straight to Richy Kreme and parked, just to have a little time to sit and talk.

Chapter 17   The Meaning of Baptism

As we sat at Richy Kreme and talked about what had just happened we both began to calm down and I would guess that our blood pressure and our pulse began to return to normal. Gradually our conversation turned to other things and I remembered the conversation that Rex and I had just had with Cordell about being saved and I was so curious about what Cordell had told us he left out of the plan of salvation.

"Jay, Rex and I went to Cordell's barber shop today and he talked to us about the plan of salvation. He showed us in the Bible where the Scriptures plainly teach that Faith is required for anyone who wants to be saved. I read for myself the verses he pointed out and one of them said that **without faith it's impossible to please God.**"

"Well, he's right about that. It's always been like that. Anywhere in the Bible you decide to read, those people who wanted to please God had to have faith in order to be obedient to what God wanted them to do. Faith has always been required, but it's never been all there was to being saved. If you read through the Old Testament you'll find Noah and Moses and Abraham and a lot of others had special jobs that God wanted them to do. But not one of them could have obeyed God without faith. So, faith is always the first thing required in order to be saved. What else did Cordell tell you?"

"Well, he pointed out some places in the Bible where the Scriptures tell us that we can't be saved without repentance. I hadn't noticed that repentance was required in order to be saved. But I had read these verses myself even before we read them with Cordell. One verse said, **except you repent, you shall all likewise perish**. How much plainer can it get than that?"

"And another verse, which I was surprised to read, said that in order to be saved we have to be willing to confess our faith in Christ with our mouths. Actually, that seems reasonable to me. How could anyone claim to be a Christian and not be willing to admit publicly that they were followers of Christ?   I can't remember where the verse was found, but I read it."

"It was Romans 10:10," Jay Thomas said. "Get that Bible in the back seat and turn to Romans 10:10."

I turned to the verse and read it out loud.

Romans 10:9 (NKJV)

9 that if you confess with your mouth the Lord Jesus and believe in your heart that God has raised Him from the dead, you will be saved.

"It says pretty plain that if we confess we'll be saved. That's about as important as anything can get."

"Yeah, and Cordell read us another verse where it says that some of the religious leaders believed on Jesus and were not saved because they were afraid to confess Him."

"That's all true, Carl. What else did you learn?"

"Well, that's where we had to leave. Cordell said there was another step required in order to be saved. He hinted that it was baptism, but every preacher I've ever asked has always said that baptism is not required in order to be saved."

"Really? What did they tell you baptism was for?"

"You know, I've asked that question several times. I asked the Baptist preacher at Victory Baptist and I asked the Methodist preacher I work for sometimes, and neither one of them had much of a reply as to the purpose of baptism. Both of them were clear about one thing though, they both agreed that baptism was not for forgiveness of sins. They said that baptism was not required in order to be saved."

"So they said that baptism doesn't save us, did they?

"OK Carl, it's time you read what the Bible has to say about the purpose of baptism. Let's start right here in 1 Peter 3:21. Read that."

1 Peter 3:20-21 (NKJV)

20 who formerly were disobedient, when once the Divine longsuffering waited in the days of Noah, while the ark was being prepared, in which a few, that is, eight souls, were saved through water.

21 There is also an antitype which now saves us--baptism (not the removal of the filth of the flesh, but the answer of a good conscience toward God), through the resurrection of Jesus Christ

"Look at what this says. First it says that Noah was saved by water. That confuses some people. After all, didn't the water destroy all life on the earth? How could it be that it saved Noah? Well it did. The reason Noah didn't die in the flood is because the water held him up while he was in the ark. There was no magic in the water. The water would have killed Noah just like it did everybody else, except for one thing. Noah had faith in God and he obeyed God's instructions to build an ark. On the one hand you could say that Noah's faith saved him, because it did. On the other hand you could say that Noah was not saved by faith alone, because it took more than faith to save him.

"You could also say that Noah was saved by works. Noah built the ark out of gopher wood just like God had told him to, and did all the things just like he was instructed by God. If he hadn't obeyed God in these works, he wouldn't have been saved. So, Noah was saved because of his obedience to God's instructions.

"And in addition to these things, Noah was saved by water. There was no miraculous magic in the water and it saved Noah because

Noah had enough faith to obey God's instructions in how to be saved. Noah would have died if the water hadn't floated the ark on the top of it. And the ark floated because Noah had enough faith to build it just like God told him to.

"Now the Bible says *'in like manner, Baptism now saves us.'*

"There's still no magic in the water. We're saved just like Noah was. Our faith saves us, just like it did Noah. And our obedience saves us the same way obedience saved Noah. We have to have enough faith to obey God's instruction for us to be saved. If we've repented of our sins and we're willing to confess our allegiance to Christ, our conscience tells us that we need to obey the rest of God's requirements to be saved. At this point we're ready to be baptized for the forgiveness of our sins.

"Peter tells us that the water is not what washes sin off our fleshly bodies, there's more to it than that. Our mind and our conscience both have to be involved in the obedience we're engaged in to be properly baptized.

"But this is not the only place in the Bible where we're told why we need to be baptized. Not by a long shot. There are plenty of other places too."

"So, the water saves us," I said. "Just like Noah was saved by water. That seems to be so simple. How is it possible for people to miss that when they read the Bible?"

"The reason they miss it is because they don't want the Bible to say it. If it did, the doctrine of *faith only* would be proved to be false. And if that happened, what would happen to their denomination? You can see why it's so important for denominational churches to deny that baptism is for the forgiveness of our sins."

"Carl, see if you can find Mark 16:16 in that Bible. Read that for us."

Mark 16:15-16 (NKJV)

15 And He said to them, "Go into all the world and preach the gospel to every creature.

16 He who believes and is baptized will be saved; but he who does not believe will be condemned.

"Here's another place where it tells us that we need to be baptized in order to be saved. Notice here that it also mentions faith? Now in this place it doesn't mention confession or repentance, but that doesn't mean that they're not required. They still are. We know they are because the Bible tells us they are in other places.

"There's another place where repentance and baptism are mentioned together like faith and baptism are here. Look at Acts 2:38."

Acts 2:38 (NKJV)

38 Then Peter said to them, "Repent, and let every one of you be baptized in the name of Jesus Christ for the remission of sins; and you shall receive the gift of the Holy Spirit.

"Now here it is again, **baptism for the remission of sins.** But this time repentance is mentioned instead of faith."

"Tell me, Jay, why did Peter not tell them they needed faith?"

"Simple, he had just preached a sermon to them with fire coming out of his head, and he told them they had killed the Christ. They had enough faith to plead with him and ask him what they needed to do to be forgiven. Peter knew they had faith and he told them to repent and be baptized for the forgiveness of their sins. In other words, people were told what to do to be saved depending on what they needed to do."

"You know, Jay, sometimes I worry about myself. I wonder if I'm really saved. I read these things in the Bible and they cause me to worry about myself.

"I know I have faith. I've always had that. And I feel sure I've repented. I've been baptized, too. I haven't confessed Christ, but I'd be willing to do that anytime. I don't know why I worry so much, but I do."

"I think I know why you worry, Carl. You know that you've been baptized, but you're questioning why you were baptized. You're wondering if you were baptized for the right reason. Does that sound pretty close?"

"Well, it could be, I guess. But tell me, if a person has been baptized, does he ever need it again?"

"Well, there is a case like that in the Bible," Jay Thomas said. "Let me see that concordance for a minute. Here it is."

Acts 19:3-5 (NKJV)
3 And he said to them, "Into what then were you baptized?" So they said, "Into John's baptism."
4 Then Paul said, "John indeed baptized with a baptism of repentance, saying to the people that they should believe on Him who would come after him, that is, on Christ Jesus."
5 When they heard this, they were baptized in the name of the Lord Jesus.

"Here's a case just like you, Carl. These people were already baptized when Paul found them, but it was the wrong kind of baptism. Look at what they did. **They were rebaptized.**"

"What do you think I should do, Jay?" I said.

"Now I'm not going to make that choice for you Carl. You have to decide what you need to do yourself. I can help you study the Bible, but this is too important for me to tell you what to do. Who knows, in a few years you might start wondering if you really understood what you did to be saved. Just like you are now."

Chapter 18   Rebaptized at Church

Cordell said he would talk to Robert Wilson, and ask him to preach about baptism on Sunday. He must have, because there couldn't have been a timelier sermon than the one he preached today.

Daddy drove me and mama to church. He never went himself but he was always willing to take us. He would be sitting in the parking lot after church to take us home. Most of the time, I went home with someone else.

I didn't have my driver's license yet but many of the young people did. I was old enough to have my license but daddy wouldn't sign the papers to let me take driving in school. He never did sign for me to get a license. The only way I was able to get them is when my brother, Cliff, signed the papers for me.

There always seemed to be someone who had the family car after church. And as many of the young people as could get in the car would take off and go somewhere. These were great times for me and this group of young people formed a bond of friendship that still exists today.

Today Robert Wilson started his sermon with this statement; "Many of you are familiar with the term *born again.* In fact, most of you are. But my question to you is this, can you teach what it means to your family members and your neighbors who need to know?"

I don't know what else he could have said that would have grabbed my attention more than this. I sure couldn't teach it, and I definitely wanted to know.

"Let's start our study this morning by looking at the Scriptures where the term *born again* is used."

"You can follow along in your Bibles if you turn to John 3.

John 3:3-5 (NKJV)

3 Jesus answered and said to him, "Most assuredly, I say to you, unless one is born again, he cannot see the kingdom of God."

4 Nicodemus said to Him, "How can a man be born when he is old? Can he enter a second time into his mother's womb and be born?"

5 Jesus answered, "Most assuredly, I say to you, unless one is born of water and the Spirit, he cannot enter the kingdom of God.

"Most of you know this story about Jesus and Nicodemus, but I want to point out what the Bible says here in verse 3. If there has ever been any question in your mind about how important it is to be born again, verse 3 should settle it once and for all. Jesus says it as plain as it can be said. **You cannot be saved unless you are born again."**

I think I already knew that part, but somehow, the way Mr. Wilson said this and the confidence he had in his voice captivated me and held me spell bound to every word. He went on to say this:

"Another thing we can see by these verses is; this is not the natural birth Jesus is talking about. Nicodemus understands that in verse 4. Being born again in a natural way would not be possible, so that tells us that Jesus is talking about another type of birth other than that."

"Now, verse 5 makes this passage so simple and so obvious that you just about have to have a false teacher to spin it in such a way to help you misunderstand it."

That last sentence struck a chord with me. Suddenly I remembered Jay Thomas' words about **the woodpecker gospel.**

"Look at the words in verse 5. Do you notice that you have to be born of the **water and the Spirit?** Look carefully at the word Spirit used here. Do you notice that this word is capitalized? That means that the Bible is talking about the Holy Spirit here. So by that alone we know that the God has a part in this new birth."

"And what about the water part here? Does that really present any problem in understanding what this is talking about? We know that this is referring to baptism. We've studied God's plan of salvation many times here and we know that in order to be saved you need faith, repentance, confession and baptism. Being born again is part of that same process."

"Verse 5 mentions being born of the water and the Spirit. There are 2 parts to the salvation process. There is the part we do and the part God does for us. Our part is to hear the gospel, have faith, repent of our sins, and be baptized. God's part is Spiritual. God changes our lives from the old sinful man who is Spiritually dead in sin, to a brand new man who is Spiritually new and free from sin."

"Now this changing to a new person process is explained again in Romans 6:4. Turn over to that verse."

As I turned to Romans 6 in Cordell's Bible, I marveled that Mr. Wilson was reading every point that he was making out of the Bible. It was so unusual for me to hear a preacher do that. This was exactly what I said I would do. I said I would never let anyone else teach me the Bible unless I could read for myself out of the Bible what they were trying to teach.

"Now, look at the words in Romans 6:2-4."

Romans 6:2-4 (NKJV)
2 Certainly not! How shall we who died to sin live any longer in it?
3 Or do you not know that as many of us as were baptized into Christ Jesus were baptized into His death?

4 Therefore we were buried with Him through baptism into death, that just as Christ was raised from the dead by the glory of the Father, even so we also should walk in newness of life.

"Look carefully at what these verses say. Verse 3 says we are baptized into Jesus' death. And verse 4 says **we are buried with Him through baptism,** and **as Christ was raised from the dead….. even so we should walk in newness of life."**

"In other words, we are born again."

"There's the physical part that we do and there's the Spiritual part that God does for us. And when Jesus said to Nicodemus, you must be born again; this is exactly what He meant."

"Now, do we need to be born again? You know the answer to that question. Yes, we must be born again in order to be saved. If anybody asks you that question now, you'll probably know more than they do about it. In fact, you can teach it now."

You know what? I could teach it now. No wonder Jay Thomas is such a good Bible teacher. All this time, he's sat and listened to this kind of Bible teaching from this church. I want that too, I thought to myself.

But Robert Wilson wasn't through with his sermon for today. He had one more point to make. This may have been the most important words anyone ever said to me in my life.

"Today I ask you," Mr. Wilson said. "Are you born again? If you are not, or if you have doubts about your salvation, don't leave this building today without making it right. If you need to respond just come down front while we all stand and sing this next song."

I knew he was talking about me. If there was anyone who had doubts about their salvation it was me.

As the song was being sung, I stepped out into the aisle and made my way to the front of the church. Mr. Wilson was there to meet me and he directed me to a front pew where we both sat down and he asked me what was wrong and how could he help me. I told him that I had been baptized in the Baptist church and I had studied until I thought I needed to be rebaptised for the forgiveness of my sins. I remember saying this, "I want to be born again, properly."

On that day I was properly baptized into Christ for the forgiveness of my sins. My old sinful self was buried with Christ and like Christ was raised from the dead by the glory of the Father, I was raised from the watery grave of baptism to walk in newness of life. I was properly ***born again.***

When the final song was sung, there was a rush forward by all the young people my age in the church. They were genuinely happy and excited for me and they couldn't wait to touch me and to shake my hand tell me how happy they were for me. Mr. Wilson was there and so was Robert Hall my Wednesday night Bible teacher. By the time it was all over, I must have shaken the hand of every person in that church.

One older lady said to me, "Angels in Heaven are rejoicing for you today, Carl." I was thankful for that old lady and I always remembered what she said to me that day. I went out of my way to try to show her a special respect when I was around her from that day on.

Chapter 19   The Magic Moment

Jay Thomas took my hand in his and with a slight grin on his face he looked at me and said, "I didn't have any doubts."

"Doubts about what," I said.

"Doubts that you'd make the right choices," he said.

"I couldn't have figured it all out without your teaching," I said. "I'd still be lost."

"Don't give me the credit," he said. "The power of salvation is in the Gospel. The Bible tells us that."

"Well, let me tell you this, you're a good friend and I appreciate all you've taught me about the Bible."

"OK, then let me tell you what you can do for me."

"What?" I said.

"You have to teach someone else the Gospel."

This was Jay Thomas' advice to me and he meant it. He lived it in his life and I was inspired by his example to try to be like that too.

Jay was a great friend.

In the beginning of my senior year in high school, a wonderful opportunity came available to me that I hadn't planned but became one of the great highlights and memories of my life. I was asked to work curb at Richy Kreme.

I met Mr. Richy at school. Not only did he own the donut/ice cream shop, he was also a member of the local school board. There was a special assembly called where some awards were given out for special achievements of the students. As I sat in the assembly watching the giving of the awards, I heard my name called. At first I was surprised to hear about an award. No one had told me that I was about to get an award.

And then I felt a tug on my arm and it was Genevieve Allen, the girl in the seat next to me. "Get up, Carl; they're calling your name."

And then the voice became clear. "The farm mechanics award goes to Carl Cooper. Come up here Carl and get your award."

I was shocked and flabbergasted. How could I get a farm mechanics award when I had taken no courses in farming in school? I wasn't even a member of the FFA. (Future Farmers of America) Something was wrong here, of that I knew.

As I hesitated to move, Genevieve pushed me up and said, "Go get your award."

I got up and went to the front and accepted the award. The crowd applauded and cheered me and they gave me a nice speech of congratulations. Thank goodness I didn't have to say anything about farm mechanics. To this day they think I am an expert on it. (Whatever it is)

Anyway, after the assembly was over, I made my way to the principal's office to turn in the award which I knew could not be mine. Mr. Richy just happened to be in the office as I got there and he congratulated me for winning the award. "Well, I'm really here to turn it in to the principal. I really didn't deserve to get it and somebody else is the one who deserves it."

"Ha!" Mr. Richy said as he walked out the door. "Smart and modest too, I like that."

He was gone before I could make a reply.

But not long after that I was notified through one of the boys at school who worked at Richy Kreme that I was asked to start working curb for the restaurant. I took the job. The pay was 40 cents per hour for the boys and 35 cents per hour for the girls. The boys had to keep the trash carried out to the dumpster.

Not only did I get paid by the hour to work there, I made money in tips too. Tips were not great. Most of the customers came from the local schools and colleges from around the county and they were not known as big tippers. A dime was a common tip and maybe once in a while I would get a quarter. During the time I worked at Richy Kreme, I always had money in my pocket.

Working at one of the hottest places in town for young people to gather when out on dates and just to come and visit their friends was a dream come true for a boy like me. I was a senior in high school and I knew everybody in school and they all knew me because of where I worked. What a great job.

I had my driver's license by the time I started working there, but our family only had one car and I very seldom got to use it. I sure couldn't afford to own one myself. Sometimes daddy let me take the car if he didn't have to work and I would pick up Rex and Linda and Jay Thomas and where do you think we would usually wind up? That's right, Richy Kreme.

One of the women who worked inside and did the cooking and filled orders had a younger sister named Doris. She was about 2 years younger than me and she was really pretty. They only lived a few hundred yards from the restaurant and sometimes Doris would walk down and visit her sister and hang around with some of us who were working curb. We had a little room made out of glass windows where we sat and waited for cars to pull up to the curb. We could see all the way around the parking lot and we would rush out and wait on the cars and take their orders.

Doris was so full of life and happy and she was fun to be around. It wasn't long before we began to see each other at school. At first, I really didn't consider her my girlfriend and besides she already had a boyfriend at school. He would meet her after class and they would stand in the halls together and talk.

I had noticed them together and sometimes I would greet her as I would happen to walk by.

But things began to change for us as she would come down to the restaurant to sit with me while I worked curb and waited on cars. We began to grow closer as we sat together and talked. One night I took off early and walked her home. Her sister, Winnie Mae, somehow caused this to happen. Mae and I were good friends and it seemed like every time an opportunity came up she would turn our conversation to her sister, Doris. Mae loved Doris. I could see that. And she wanted everything to be just wonderful for her. Looking back on it, I'm pretty sure I was set up by Mae to walk her sister home.

It was almost 10:30 when we left the restaurant heading for Doris' house. Neither one of us was in any hurry for the walk to be over. We took our time and we walked slow, stopping every few feet to hold hands and laugh about something silly that had happened at school. We stopped about half way and we stood looking at each other and holding hands.

"I told Mae I wanted you to walk me home," she said.

"So, you gals kidnapped me, did you," I said.

"Are you sorry?" she said looking right into my eyes.

Her face got closer to mine and I could see that she wanted me to kiss her. I held her close and she held me and we embraced. I remember that kiss even today. I think it was at that moment, for the first time in my life that I fell completely in love.

I think it happened to her just as it did for me. It was after 11 by the time we made it to her porch. We stood there for a long time and I couldn't bring myself to leave. Doris held me close and didn't want to turn me loose and go inside the house. The spell was broken by her mother. She waited as long as she could for her daughter to come in, and she opened the door and called.

This night was a magic moment for me. It changed my life. She was so perfect and beautiful and I couldn't get her off my mind.

But the next day at school, the magic in my world evaporated and fell apart. As the last class bell rang and it was time to go home, I walked out across the campus and I just happened to walk past the auditorium entrance and I stopped. I was face to face with Doris and her boyfriend standing together on the auditorium steps. I'm not sure what she saw in my face, and it almost looked like she wanted to say something to me. But it was no use and too late, I walked away. I was mad and I was hurt. At that moment, an unconscious decision was made by me never to see her again. It would have been exactly like that except for one thing. Doris didn't wait for me to leave her. By the time I got home our phone was already ringing and it was her. We made up. She was leaving her boyfriend for me and she pledged her love for me. We have been together ever since.

Doris and I spent every minute together that we could. We went places together, we dated with Jay Thomas and Linda and we went to church together. Like me, she had been a Baptist and had been baptized in the Baptist church before we met. She absorbed what she heard like a sponge. Between me, Jay Thomas and Linda and what she heard at church, she was baptized for the remission of her sins when she was 17 years old.

Chapter 20   My Stupid Attempt To Evangelize

I knew that Jay Thomas was right when he said I needed to teach the gospel to someone else. I made it my goal to try to find a way to do that.

Teaching the gospel is like sowing seed in a field. Every seed you scatter won't come up and grow, but some will. Who knows how long it will take a seed to germinate and grow, but the more seeds that are scattered the more chances we have of one taking root.

The Bible calls the Word of God *"The Seed."*

Luke 8:5-8 (NKJV)

5 A sower went out to sow his seed. And as he sowed, some fell by the wayside; and it was trampled down, and the birds of the air devoured it.

6 Some fell on rock; and as soon as it sprang up, it withered away because it lacked moisture.

7 And some fell among thorns, and the thorns sprang up with it and choked it.

8 but others fell on good ground, sprang up, and yielded a crop a hundredfold.

Luke 8:11 (NKJV)

11 "Now the parable is this: The seed is the word of God.

The Bible tells us that the seed is the word of God and we need to sow as much of it as we can. All of it won't germinate and grow but some will. There is also a very important principle here about creating Christians.

If you planted a wheat seed what would you expect to come up? You would expect to see wheat come up, right? The same would be true if you planted corn seed or cotton.

The same is true when the pure Word of God is planted in the hearts of men. The plant that springs forth is a Christian. The same kind of Christian that the Apostle Paul was and the same kind of Christians that the original disciples were. If the same unaltered seed (Word of God) is planted today, then the plant that springs forth is an identical plant to the very first Christian described in the Bible. This is how pure unaltered Christianity spreads from generation to generation.

Do you wonder why there are so many different kinds of churches in existence today? How is it that there are so many denominations out there teaching different doctrines that actually contradict each other? How would it make any common sense for all of them to be right and acceptable to God when they teach different things?

Well, they can't. Such division as that totally violates Jesus' final prayer to God as He prayed, knowing He was about to die on the cross. Look at this Scripture.

John 17:20-21 (NKJV)
20 "I do not pray for these alone, but also for those who will believe in Me through their word;
21 that they all may be one, as You, Father, are in Me, and I in You; that they also may be one in Us, that the world may believe that You sent Me.

Notice who Jesus is praying for in verse 20. He is not only praying for His disciples but He expands His prayer to include all people who would believe on Him through their word. That includes you and me and anyone who is influenced to have faith because of the Bible.

And then look at what Jesus wants to happen in verse 21. Jesus wants every Christian to be united. And not just "somewhat united," but united as God and Jesus are united.

This means that they teach the same thing and they both teach the true Word of God.

Teaching different gospels and different doctrine is wrong. It totally violates Jesus' prayer the night He was about to die on the cross.

It also prevents the true Word of God from being sown in the hearts of men. If divided doctrine is sown in the hearts of men then the seed that is being sown has been altered and is not the true seed. The plant that springs forth will not be the original Christian but will be the genetically altered Christian. Baptist seed will produce Baptists. Methodist seed will produce Methodists. Only the true, unaltered seed will produce the original Christians that were produced on the day of Pentecost when the first gospel sermon was preached in Acts chapter 2.

How easy is it to find the true seed being taught, you might ask? If you've read this far in this book you already know that my search was not easy. Yours may not be either. But the Bible tells us to *"work out our own salvation."* And it also says that the path to Heaven is narrow and hard to find and there will be few who find it.

Philippians 2:12 (NKJV)
12 Therefore, my beloved, as you have always obeyed, not as in my presence only, but now much more in my absence, work out your own salvation with fear and trembling;

Matthew 7:14 (NKJV)
14 Because narrow is the gate and difficult is the way which leads to life, and there are few who find it.

An opportunity came up at the Maryville Church of Christ to help in an evangelistic campaign.

Both Jay Thomas and I were eager to help.

There was a plan for the Gatlinburg Church of Christ to survey the community and announce a gospel meeting that was about to be held. The Maryville Church volunteered to help with this effort and spread the word in the community. The young people were given the more rural areas because we had more energy to walk the mountain hillsides.

The plan was this: take a survey sheet with you and a flyer announcing the meeting. Ask a few questions about their religious affiliation and then give them a flyer.

Now this was a good plan. Who would have thought that anyone could mess it up, right? But I did.

I made many stops at houses and for the most part things went well. But the one that didn't still haunts me in my bed at night when things are quiet and still and I have time to think and remember.

I was pretty far out of town and I had walked up a dirt driveway to an old ramshackle house just past a hog lot that was in much need of repair. There were only 3 or 4 hogs in the lot but it smelled pretty bad. There were 3 young boys about 10 or 12 years old sitting on the front porch with their feet dangling through the loose and busted banisters. Their faces were dirty and they were ragged and they watched me come up the driveway without saying a word.

"Hey guys!" I said. "I'm with the Gatlinburg Church of Christ. I'm taking a religious survey. I wonder if I could ask you a couple of questions." No one on the porch moved. There was no reply.

"Do you guys go to church?" I said.

There was no reply and it made me nervous it was so unusual.

"Well thanks anyway," I said and I handed a flyer about the meeting to the nearest boy and he seemed reluctant to take something from me, but he finally did.

"I'll see you guys," I said. And I turned to leave.

"Anne does," he said.

"What was that?" I said as I turned back to see who spoke.

"He said Anne does," one of the boys said.

"Oh, you mean Anne goes to church? Is Anne here?"

One of the boys got up and opened the screen door to the house and hollered, "Anne, this man out here wants to see you."

Anne came to the door and held the screen door only slightly open where she could see me out through the crack. She was a young teenage girl only slightly younger than me. Her dress was torn in places and like the boys, she needed a good bath. She was pretty underneath that tangled mess of hair, I could see that.

"What do you want?" she said.

"Well, I'm taking a religious survey and I just wanted to ask you a couple of questions if I can."

"What kind of questions?" she said, somewhat nervously.

"Well, like do you go to church, is one?"

"Why are you asking us these questions?" she said.

"Well the church is trying to find out how many people go to church," I said. I guess I thought that was the truth when I said it. By now I had forgot the real reason was to try to encourage people to attend the gospel meeting that was coming up. The only thing I was concentrating on now was getting these questions on this page answered so I could go.

"Do you go to church?" I said again.

"Annie goes to church," one of the boys said. "Tell him Annie."

"Sure, I go to church," Annie said.

I checked off the first question on the list. "What kind is it?" I asked.

"What do you mean?" Annie said.

"I mean what kind of church is it?" I said.

"What do you mean what kind?" she said. I could see the nervousness in her actions and I could hear it in her voice.

"I mean what kind is it?" I said. I didn't have sense enough just to spare her the humiliation of not being able to answer this question about church. I just kept pressing the point, asking for an answer.

"What kind is it? What's the name of the denomination?"

By this time her fingers were trembling on the door.

"Gospel," she said. "Gospel."

I laughed. What kind of a person am I? **I laughed.**

She broke down in tears and she covered her face and she closed the door and ran. She hid from me and she never would come back out to the door again.

I saw instantly what I had done. I humiliated that poor girl. What a fool I was to laugh at her like that.

This is a word to the readers of this book. If you ever get a chance to knock on someone's door to tell them about the gospel. Remember, if you can't do it with humility and compassion, don't do it at all.

I told Jay Thomas what had happened and all that had taken place. He understood, but there was nothing we could do to take it back.

This episode is still just as fresh on my mind today as it was then. I can't tell you how much this bothers me. Even now!

JAMES 2:19-24 (NKJV)

19 You believe that there is one God. You do well. Even the demons believe--and tremble! But do you want to know, O foolish man, that faith without works is dead?

20. Was not Abraham our father justified by works when he offered Isaac his son on the altar? Do you see that faith was working together with his works, and by works faith was made perfect? And the Scripture was fulfilled which says, "Abraham believed God, and it was accounted to him for righteousness." And he was called the friend of God.

24 You see then that a man is justified by works, and not by faith only.

Made in the USA
Columbia, SC
04 May 2022

59742931R10078